"Berri Meyers offers a clear, practical guide to strategic planning — why you need it, how to do it, and how to make it work. If more businesses and organizations learn these lessons, they will clean-up fewer mistakes."

> —John P. Walters, former Cabinet member and Director, White House Office of National Drug Control Policy and Executive Vice President, the Hudson Institute

Colonel Meyers has written nothing less than a great book on strategic planning. And why wouldn't he? He's walked this walk, learning from mistakes and great successes. He was the top organizational development officer...one of the most respected planning leaders in the entire state government....all a CEO, Executive Director or Governor needs: the book is clear, researched, linear, and maybe most importantly, outlines the traps, false-shortcuts, and mis-steps that can avoid disaster and ensure success. Wished I'd read it 15 years ago!

> —Daniel Granholm Mulhern, Michigan's First Gentleman and author of *Everyday Leadership: Getting Results in Business, Politics, and Life*

"Insightful, an easily understood tutorial for a planning process absent in far too many organizations! This is a great strategic planning text for colleges and universities. Timely and well focused..."

> —Mike Flanagan, State Superintendent of Schools, Michigan

"Colonel Meyers has written a superb guide to strategic planning that accomplishes the seemingly impossible: it explains both the "why" and the "how" of strategic planning in a compact, readable volume. His informal style coupled with detailed step-by-step processes (with valuable tips and advice from his deep pool of experiences as a planner) will benefit all groups of planners. Use of this book will assure that the uninitiated will comprehend the planning process, that the elite professionals will expedite their planning process while the reluctant majority of us — who engage in strategic planning like they pay insurance premiums — dreading the future rather than embracing its opportunities — will gain future insight and increased current productivity."

— **Brigadier General Michael McDaniel**, former Assistant Adjutant General for Homeland Security, Michigan and former Homeland Security Advisor for Michigan

Strategic Planning:

Clean Up in Aisle 4!

Strategic Planning:

Clean Up in Aisle 4!

Finally A Roadmap For Achieving Your Organizational Vision

Berri K. Meyers

ISBN: 978-0-692-00571-2

For more information, please contact:

b.k. meyers & associates, LLC

517-322-0116

berrimeyers@comcast.net

www.bkmeyersandassociates.com

Library of Congress Cataloging-in-Publication Data

Meyers, Berri K., 1952-

Strategic planning, clean up in aisle 4! : finally a roadmap for achieving your organizational vision / Berri K. Meyers.

p. cm.

ISBN 978-0-692-00571-2

1. Strategic planning. 2. Management. I. Title.

HD30.28.M4935 2009

658.4'012--dc22

2009040208

Manufactured in the United States of America

CONTENTS

INTRODUCTION

Is there any better way to visualize a task-at-hand that few organizations want to venture into, than that universal call heard in the busiest of places, "CLEAN UP IN AISLE FOUR!"? Strategic planning has been deferred or ignored in every corner of industry and organizational development often because the process is misunderstood. Almost no one wants to be asked, or tasked to the process of strategic planning—often perceived as a dry and difficult process. True strategy is best defined as a plan or method for employing stratagems, or strategies to achieve various goals. An amalgam of various processes, theories and practices frame this process we categorize as strategic planning.

This text clarifies the most misunderstood of all planning processes—strategic planning. An absolute essential foundation for organizational continuity, strategic direction and growth in every organization. The most dynamic type of plans—strategic plans are often absent because people are intimidated by the strategic planning process. This text explains and illuminates the various steps, prescribes a logical sequence and highlights the common pitfalls for a strategic planning process. This methodology is *applicable to all organizations*. It is simple, effective and easy for your leadership team to implement. I outline the practices and procedures I use with clients, not theoretical ideas no one has tested. I know you will find these valuable and effective. You may ask, *why didn't we do this before now?*

A dozen different ways to create strategic plans are postulated by 100's of practitioners, all different and equally confusing and incomplete. Only the strategically astute and proactive senior leaders cite the value strategic planning has added to their organization. Sometimes the positive impacts created by great strategic plans are mal-credited to other organizational initiatives. It can be difficult to know the best way to approach this essential process.

I have been fortunate in my professional experience to observe the positive impacts a well prepared strategic plan can have on an organization. I have seen strategic plans transition organizations from mediocre-performing to *best in class*. I have seen organizational cultures mature from routine and average to exciting working environments, dynamic organizational cultures that attract new people, new ideas and create exuberance. My experience developing strategic plans in private and public-sector organizations, has given me a special perspective for strategic planning. While strategic planning can create great and positive impacts for organizations, it can also create welcome and meaningful impacts for the team members investing their lives in those same organizations.

I have been very fortunate to have worked for exciting leaders, which allowed me to apply the principles and techniques of strategic planning, acquired through graduate studies and hands-on experience. I was able to observe the impacts, hear the responses and gage the improvements strategic planning can have on an organization. I was able to modify standard methods and procedures and then track the results of these changes. My annual surveys of team members allowed me to document the perceptions and beliefs employees held for the impact they felt was created by an innovative strategic plan.

As I facilitate the development of strategic plans for numerous clients I see the critical impetus strategic planning can be for transitioning a simple organizational *climate* change into a systemic *cultural* change. Strategic planning in its best form is a team-based endeavor.

Those readers with some experience in strategic planning principles and processes are looking for the difference in the unique strategic planning process I prescribe. What specifically within this text is so notable? What are the significant differences that set this tutorial above the many volumes already available? Much of my suggested strategic planning process will seem similar to the strategic planning process taught by the American Management Association, which is certainly a great planning process, or even similar to graduate business curriculums. Several key aspects of the strategic planning I prescribe in this text will jump out as different and notable. Deliberate linkage to organizational budget processes, measurable metrics that capture organizational performance and a specific deployment process will set this prescriptive process apart from others. In addition, you will begin to understand how a strategic planning process weaves leadership, discipline and motivation into a comprehensive performance formula.

It is this *25% difference* from basic strategic planning processes that is noteworthy and valuable. The real performance edge derived by following my guidelines will justify your re-reading and endorsement to others. I outline the simple, inter-linked steps for you to follow — then emphasize important implications and impacts that can ratchet-up your organization through significant achievements. I mean *really* significant achievements! I urge you to read this text as a strategic planning *process*, not an event.

This is a quick-read, process-centric text that can leverage your existing leadership assets, jump-start your team energy and get your organization moving towards real growth. I provide the road map and waypoints for you to follow, as you apply the context of *your organizational world*. You provide the leadership. After reading this book you may apply leadership to your organization in a different way. You must provide the enthusiasm and energy needed for this grand endeavor. You and your team, a team chosen with a clear understanding of the implications in the composition of such teaming, will determine your direction, rate-of-march and ultimate end-state. This process, when applied as I present it, will be effective for *any* organization, in *any* market. It doesn't matter if your organization is educational, private-sector business, government, military or not-for-profit.

From my experience, many organizations are hoping for the silver bullet that can energize organizational change or create the real growth desired. While we all know no 'silver bullet' exists, this text will come as close as any solution possible. This process may be the best investment you have made in changing your management focus and leadership style. If you seek only incremental change this text may be of limited help for you. However if you seek to *transform* your organization, creating growth or change many times your routine annual progress, this book will serve you well. The keys to greater success *lie in your application and discipline to the process* and in your dedication to change your organizational practices, in accordance with my strategic planning process and other suggestions I present.

My leadership and management experience, in industrial, governmental and military planning, have forged the refinement of this strategic planning process. I will also highlight the impacts these changes will drive. The increase in your team member's energy and morale, which this process can generate, will surprise you. Increased team synergy, at every level of the organization will add tremendous value. Once you galvanize the members of your organization on a common set of goals and objectives the results can be monumental. When your organizational behaviors are truly aligned with sound Values and you have set everyone moving in the same direction, your team's accomplishments are limitless. Once set in motion you will be left to only *motivate and inspire* the people driving your success.

The multiple impacts on your team members must be a serious consideration in strategic planning efforts. These impacts are overlooked by most strategic planning authors and tutorials. Is your organization really ready and actually willing to embark in such a proactive direction? I ask this question because sometimes people don't fully realize the responsibilities and heightened expectations created by change. Many organizations feel like they are ready, they truly believe their people are poised for positive action, without truly understanding everything that entails. Will the senior leaders in your organization really stop their activities momentarily to celebrate team accomplishments? I mean really stop and celebrate. You and *all of your senior leaders* must be willing to embrace the implications of dramatic change on team members and actually be willing to change the policies and attitudes to support your team where needed.

I can provide the provocative questions. I can outline the step-by-step process. I can shed light on the impacts you will create. You must understand the real essence of your organization's transformation lies in the *leadership demonstrated* by those rallying your organizational energies and creativity. I can only incite you to question your status quo, your strategic direction. *You* must be the catalyst to transition your *new organizational climate* into a *new organizational culture*.

ONE

A FRAME OF REFERENCE

Strategic planning in the most general sense is a specific planning process aimed to achieve prescribed goals, accomplished through the intermediary achievement of specific objectives, using distinct and prescribed strategies. It is a very specific type of plan in the hierarchy of formal plans, nestled between near-term plans (shorter in scope) and long-range plans (longer in scope). Strategic plans are designed for achievement within a three-year to five-year window from commencement. In comparison, long-range plans are generally five-years to twenty-years in focus, are often general in nature and lack the specificity of strategic plans. Near-term plans are usually six to 24 months in focus, lack formal metrics for monitoring progress and use only basic 'tracking' measures to determine status.

Strategic plans identify end-states through one or more goals using mandatory strategic objectives as interim accomplishments. Strategic objectives are designed to be mandatory requirements to achieve the desired goal. Therefore if any one of the strategic objectives is not fully achieved, the end-stated goal cannot be fully achieved. Additionally, the

1

means for achieving these objectives are prescribed as specific strategies. Each goal will include one or more supporting strategic objectives and each strategic objective will include one or more supporting strategies. Later I will discuss how such objectives are accomplished by outlining the Action Plan process unique to each work-team.

WHY BUILD A STRATEGIC PLAN?

Why should an organization build a strategic plan? Couldn't they achieve their goals without a formal plan? The answer is probably not, or at least not with any certainty. There are just too many personalities, variables and interpretations of direction to align the organization through less formal means. A well written strategic plan will provide several things few senior leaders can provide for their organizations, without the structure of a strategic plan. Think of a strategic plan as the architect's final drawings, the blueprints, the materials list and the assembly instructions codified in one manual for success. Could we build a house without these things—sure, but you can imagine what the results might look like.

FAIR EXPECTATIONS

What can you fairly expect from a properly developed strategic plan? Several expectations can be satisfied by a good strategic plan. Let's clarify what we are talking about. What do I mean by a *good* strategic plan? A good strategic plan is a strategic plan built using a prescribed methodology, such as the one I outline in this text. This includes a formal process of using metrics for measuring progress/regress relative to stated objectives. It also includes a formalized process for linking the strategic plan to the organizational resourcing or budgetary process. These are reasonable and fair expectations:

REASONABLE AND FAIR
EXPECTATIONS

- Greater clarity of organizational direction.
- A better understanding of organizational priorities.
- Team members aligned with organizational Values and the organizational Mission, working towards achieving the organizational Vision.
- Resource and budgetary priorities aligned with organizational tasking priorities.
- Team members that feel more 'in tune' with senior leader's expectations.
- Team members will better understand their team and individual 'fit' with corporate goals.
- The organizational *culture* will transition over time to reflect organizational values.

VALUE ADDED

What value does strategic planning provide? Sound strategic planning will codify your organization's strategic direction for customers, stakeholders and team members. Sound strategic planning will also galvanize the focus and interest of organizational team members and align their efforts towards desired end-states in a way that improves resource utilization. In effect, a strategic plan that is correctly developed and properly deployed will start a *culture* change throughout your organization. Don't confuse this with a *climate* change. It makes little sense for organizations to leave-it-to-chance for their team members, shareholders and customers to figure out the correct priorities, assign appropriate resources and hope for success.

A Responsibility of the Senior Leader

Who within the organization does strategic planning? Who is responsible for accomplishing such a vast project? Chapter 3 discusses specific planning team development and composition but it is important to understand senior leaders conduct strategic planning at the highest level of the organization. This is not something you delegate to a committee or pass on to a few high level assistants operating in isolation. *Strategic planning is a team sport* and it must be accomplished by the most senior leadership in the organization. The ultimate responsibility for strategic planning belongs to the Chief Executive Officer. I have seen several organizations affix this responsibility to other senior leaders, lower level committees or even a specific individual for development in isolation. Without exception, these ventures have ended in miserable failure. I cannot understate the importance of the organization's most senior leader's personal commitment and involvement in this critical effort. Yes, I said involvement. I don't mean, "keep me briefed on this project each week" or "keep me informed, not involved." I am talking about the President, the Chairman of the Board, the CEO, etc., personally attending every planning session and spearheading the deployment of your Strategic Plan to every member of the organization. Yes, regardless of the number team members, I mean to say *every* member of your organization. The strategic planning process must cascade from the central leader to rank and file team members. Now you are beginning to understand the genesis for the holistic impact a strategic plan will have on an organization.

A Precise Process for All Organizations

This book is intended to de-mystify the most essential of all planning processes—strategic planning. An absolute essential foundation for organizational continuity, direction and growth in every organization, yet the most misunderstood and seemingly mysterious elements—strategic plans are often absent because people are intimidated by the strategic planning process. This text will clarify and illuminate the various steps, their logical sequence and shed light on the common pitfalls in a strategic planning process *appli cable to all organizations.* It is simple, effective and easy for your leadership team to implement. I think you will find it valuable and effective. You will ask yourself, *why didn't we do this before now?*

TWO

VISION, MISSION AND VALUES . . . OR IS IT?

I t is important to understand the foundation for strategic planning and how it supports the cornerstones of any organization. A strategic plan is a well defined, specific roadmap, stated in goals and supporting objectives, to move an organization towards its Vision. Strategic planning is an incremental overlapping *process* of achieving prescribed goals and supporting objectives through a systematic effort that aligns team and team-member efforts in achieving the organizational Vision. I describe it as an overlapping *process* because strategic planning must be a living regenerative process whereby new goals and strategic objectives are added as accomplishments dictate. It is a *process*, not an event. Strategic planning is set apart from most other types of planning because it must be dynamic in nature, not static. Strategic plans that are inconsiderate of their dynamic, ever-changing strategic environments, are simply too rigid to endure. CEOs offices are filled with strategic plans that have never been deployed or implemented because they were obsolete by the time these plans were published or simply out-paced by a changing business environment.

7

VISION: Most organizations have a Vision as a hypothetically desired end-state. Usually it is short and clear leaving little to interpretation. Simply, it summarizes the ideal direction or destination of the organization and ideally is held up as a guiding light for everyone to strive for. It is what you hope to become. Based upon this azimuth-indicating guidance it becomes the starting point for strategic planning. Normally the Vision is stated, then a supporting Mission is crafted that supports the organization's movement towards the stated Vision. Vision first, then the supporting Mission. Sometimes an organization is already in motion, possibly the forward progress is only slight, then a new CEO or President crafts a new Vision. How does this work? Yes, it can be a problem although well intended. In these cases usually a new Mission must also be crafted to clarify how the organization will move towards its new Vision.

The exceptions to this sequence are military organizations and some private-sector third-party service organizations. In these exceptions the Mission is dictated by a higher authority or statute or a single-focus customer whereupon the Vision then becomes the interpretive lens for implementing the Mission. In these unusual situations it becomes Mission first, then interpretative Vision. A well written Vision should paint a picture for stakeholders, customers and team members of *where we hope to go.*

MISSION: The Mission for most organizations is a clearly stated purpose detailing what the organization does or tries to do, essentially why the organization exists. It may include major emphasis areas from the Chief Executive Officer. It differs from the Vision in that it is not conceptual and ideal, rather an empirical practice, process, service or function that can explain the organization's reason to exist. In contrast the Vision may be much more conceptual, broad scoped or idealistic. The Mission describes the present, the Vision describes the future end-state. A well written Mission should inform stakeholders, customers and team members *what it is we do or hope to do.*

VALUES: Values are selected and defined to establish the key tenets of the organization's moral constitution. These should be the hallmarks of organizational behaviors. Values should speak volumes about what is important to the organization as it executes its organizational Mission in support of the Vision. Values should be the *proof points* for validating all organizational behaviors, both in policy, practice and process. Senior leaders must make decisions, act and demonstrate such Values in every context of their business. Deviations from this essential practice are easily observed by everyone in the organization—the single largest reason for the erosion of senior leader creditability. This fundamental has no boundaries, exceptions or sector-unique qualifications. It is incredibly important Values are chosen carefully and specifically. When you select, or re-validate the organizational Values it is key to identify Values, not just end-states that allude to real Values.

How These Cornerstones Move Us Forward

Vision, Mission and Values present an incredibly large opportunity for leaders to galvanize the spirit and energies of an organization. When employees can see the organizational Vision and understand their contribution within the Mission, attitudes and energies become refreshed. Only when every team member 'sees themselves in the picture' can their total talents and creativities be realized. This is one of most over-looked opportunities by senior leaders in strategic planning. When leaders provide the targets, the tools and the motivations—mountains can be moved!

Vision, Mission and Values are also the conduits that connect fragmentary organizations. Where organizations are designed as vertical, having one central leader — or horizontal, having many central leaders — the Vision establishes the strategic direction *connection* common to all elements. Where geography or dissimilar Missions create separation between organizational sub-elements, common Vision and Values bind these sub-elements to achieve a unified strategic direction. In this way, strategic plans created for major sub-elements *are nested by sharing a common strategic direction* while still subject to different resource influences, Mission direction and leadership. In this way we are *strategically nesting* our direction (alignment) with the greater organization's intent (Vision) for all stakeholders.

CLIMATE VS. CULTURE

Everyone can relate to the subtle, or maybe larger, changes the most recent replacement supervisors brought. Changing the *climate* in an organization is as easy as walking over and turning off the lights. Climate changes are defined as transitory, temporary or cosmetic changes that often only have similar impact on the organizational work environment. Sometimes climate changes are helpful and even necessary but they remain small elements in moving an organization forward.

Changing to improve the *organizational culture* is the silver bullet that only the highest-achieving organizations have accomplished. In the most extreme cases of success, corporate cultures have been achieved that unlock the creativity, energy and talent of every team member. You have read about some of these examples. Tom Peters, the noted author and motivational speaker for excellence has crafted a reputation for hallmarking such organizations. These organizations, where forward progress has been measured in miles not inches, have been successful in changing their *culture*. Vision, Mission and Values establish the parameters for just such a cultural change.

Getting the foundation pieces just right is more involved and important than first meets the eye. I am often met with glazed stares and disbelief when I meet with clients to discuss their strategic planning journey. CEOs are amazed to hear we might spend an entire day with their senior leadership team just redefining, rewording and getting consensus on updated **Vision, Mission** and **Values** elements. Don't make the common mistake of globing onto the nucleus of a Vision or Mission statement just because it is something the boss jotted onto a cocktail napkin during a *blinding flash of genius*. Rarely do these 'pet rocks' meet the test for well written Vision or Mission statements. There are some basic rules to follow in developing such things — IF you are to harvest the most from this essential triad of the organization's future.

A FEW BASIC RULES

VISION, MISSION AND VALUES

Bear in mind these key elements when developing or updating your Vision, Mission and Values. Use clear and concise statements. Make certain these things are clear to readers that are unfamiliar with your organization. Envision a new employee or supplier that is not familiar with your organization's purpose, history or direction. The age-old KISS principle (Keep It Simple Stupid) applies here.

VISION

- r̲aints the picture of the desired or future end-state.
- Ideally it is motivating, compelling and better than the present state of the organization.
- Should be achievable and credible.
- Durable, very little change over time.
- Futuristic and enlightening.

MISSION

- Answers the What, How, Why and for Whom.
- States or alludes to the purpose of the organization.
- What is it that we do?
- General focus, *not* measured.
- May be shaped by special emphasis.
- Answers the question — why do we exist?

VALUES

- Expressed *pictures* of what *good* looks like.
- Essential beliefs of the organization.
- Enduring, should not change greatly with leadership changes.
- Speaks to the desired *culture* –not just to *climate.*
- Must be demonstrated in deed, policy and action by all.
- Key focus points for openly sharing.
- Should be defined using demonstrated behaviors.
- Ideally are indelible and consistent, horizontally and vertically throughout the organization.

Vision, Mission and Values should be discussed often during team member gatherings. Employees must hear examples of what these things look like from the most senior leaders—and often! Sharing and discussing these elements will focus people in their transition of understanding about where, how, when and by whom organizational change is occurring. Whether during a quarterly town-hall meeting, staff meetings or customer presentations, the more often these sacred underpinnings are talked about the greater the rally point for organizational energy. Institutionalizing the Vision, Mission and Values through placards, pocket cards, newsletters and bulletin boards brings employees together. Imagine that the US Army has distributed small plastic tags for wearing on soldier's dog-tags that outline the US Army Values. This is the leading edge of organizational *alignment*. As simple as it seems, nothing will shape the direction of effort and priorities for support, as well as the senior leadership sharing these insightful 'pictures.'

Vision, Mission and Values are excellent topics for warming up group discussions—even routine meetings. Using these as springboards for gathering everyone's attention and sharing stories of how senior leaders are using these same principles in their corporate actions guides employee thinking and actions. Many years ago I learned, "people will supervise—as they are supervised." An organization I spent many years with made it mandatory *to link every training session or group discussion* by verbalizing the linkage to the organization's Vision, Mission or Values. Anytime we spoke to a group of team members, our introductory comments were required to be linked to the organization's Vision, Mission or Values and the training at hand, or the purpose of the gathering. Using this process, the Vision, Mission and Values were institutionalized throughout the organization in just one year. A fairly impressive accomplishment for a horizontal organization spread across 60 cities with over 9,000 team members.

ALIGNMENT

Organizational alignment includes more than a mere similarity in intentions or direction. Alignment includes ensuring organizational behaviors are *aligned* with the organizational Values and the Vision or direction. Likewise, the organizational behaviors of all subordinate or supplemental elements, as in horizontal and fragmented vertical organizations, must be congruent and true to the Vision and Values of the organization.

Aligning an organization requires a multitude of efforts and a common focus. Organizational alignment is also multi-dimensional. It is more than just pointing everyone in a similar strategic direction. A thorough understanding of the organizational Vision, Mission and Values are only 50% of real alignment success. Complete organizational alignment is more than just providing guidance in the form of Vision, Mission and Values. These codified cornerstones are only foundational elements that provide a framework for other alignment essentials.

ACTIONS

Organizational *actions* must reflect the organizational Values in deed, policy and actions. Actions of the organization itself must reflect the Values and support the Vision of the organization. Plant closings, employee lay-offs, selling off major Divisions — do these major organizational actions reflect the promises of last month, last week — or the Values and Vision of the organization? If you've observed leaders talking one storyline and walking a different storyline, then you know what I am talking about. John Baldoni's, *180 Ways to Walk the Leadership Talk* and Dave Cottrell's *Listen Up Leader* are both excellent texts illustrating this observance in leadership credibility—a key part of organizational alignment. Harvey and Lucia's text, *144 Ways To WALK THE TALK* further illuminates this observable link in alignment.

BEHAVIORS

Both *organizational* behaviors and *individual* behaviors are highly visible indicators of organizational alignment. Some would tell us organizations don't have *behaviors.* I suggest they do and in many situations they reflect the real agenda or obscure intentions unknown to rank and file team members. Transparency and forthrightness-of-action can be positive signs of strategic direction and honesty within an organization. The US Army uses a core of Inspectors General to act as honest brokers, ensuring organizational actions, organizational behaviors and individual behaviors reflect the Values and Vision of their organization.

Individual behaviors must also support and mirror the codified Values of every organization. The National Football League spends considerable time and effort to ensure all NFL players portray the correct organizational image, through individual behaviors both on and off the football field. Large home-based sales organizations, selling home-caring products, nutritional aids and cosmetics spend considerable efforts in personnel training so their *business owner-sales agents* project the right corporate image, although technically the sales personnel own their own separate businesses.

In the past few years we've read and heard about the reported actions and behaviors of corporate giants like Enron, Tyco and others where individual behaviors and organizational behaviors defied the organizational Values, bilking tens of millions of dollars from investors, employees and suppliers. Therefore in order to achieve total organizational alignment there must be true congruency between the actions and Values of an organization, to include consistent demonstrated behaviors of those Values reflected in **both organizational and individual actions**, policies and deeds.

THREE

BUILDING YOUR PLANNING TEAM

Selecting your strategic planning team is the start of your formal strategic planning journey. I said earlier strategic planning is a team sport and it really is for several reasons. Your team should be dynamic and change somewhat with time. I recommend you stabilize it for the first two years while you mature your plan through development, deployment, execution and your first annual revision. There are a dozen theories about the specifics of planning team composition. These variances range from using a vertical slice of the organization, from the CEO to entry-level team members, while other practitioners extol value in selecting a cross-sectional group based on gender, ethnicity, experience and levels of position within the organization. All of these various methods have their particular merits and trade-offs. It might be more useful to understand the various impacts on your strategic planning process as it applies to your organization.

LEVELS OF PLANNING SCOPE

Keep in mind in this text we are talking about building a strategic plan, *not* an operational or tactical level plan. Therefore, it will be more useful to select team members that can think, visualize and conceptualize at the strategic level. It is tempting and prudent to choose personnel from all walks of the organization when trying to be inclusive of all team members. Inclusion is critical in every organization but the time for it within the strategic planning context comes after the first 18-24 months of planning maturity. Is it really fair to expect an entry-level employee to keep pace with conversations that discuss the organization's history with specific policies and how they may have been off-target accomplishing their intended goals? Would employees from *every level* of the organization be the best choice or are we really suggesting it might be best to have representatives from *every area* of the organization? This is a better picture.

PLANNING SCOPE DURATION

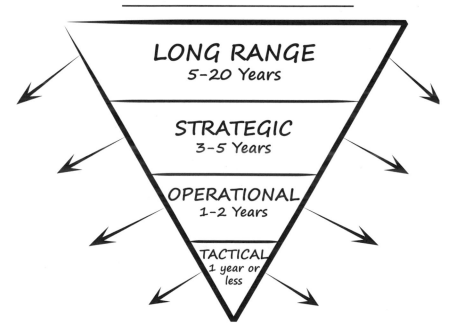

LONG RANGE
5-20 Years

STRATEGIC
3-5 Years

OPERATIONAL
1-2 Years

TACTICAL
1 year or less

Select personnel that can effectively represent every functional and geographic area of your organization. Yes, this includes organized labor representatives, informal groups that represent larger numbers of employees within the organization and geographically separated employee groups. It should include all of the senior level leaders — yes even the recalcitrant seniors who vow to never accept any new ideas. It absolutely must include the President, CEO, COO or what ever title has been placed at the top of your organizational pyramid. Be inclusive in this team selection through functional-area representation, not by your personal comfort-zones, good-ole-boys or favorite sons. Some readers will muse at this mention, but there are serious reasons to understand why I do so. Think about it within the context of your own organization.

Planning Team Composition

If you know you have shortfalls in senior leader representation of your organization with regard to particular groups of employees, by gender or ethnicity for example, select the most experienced people from these groups that are on the fringe of becoming senior leaders. You and they will prosper by their inclusion. You need their perspective as you grow your organization towards your Vision. If you have shortfalls in labor-management relationship building, this is a great time to include additional representatives from your labor organizations. Be proactive — ensure the personnel you select have real experience with your organization.

Sullivan and Harper, in their text *Hope Is Not A Method* suggests senior leaders at the strategic level of an organization should spend most of their working time each week thinking and acting in the strategic realm — something very few leaders actually do. Why not? It's simply not their comfort-zone. Most senior leaders *paid their dues* at the tactical and operational levels of their organization or in previous assignments with other organizations. Many have convinced themselves they are very good while operating at these levels and clearly their success and rise to their present positions underscores their beliefs. The problem at hand is — they are now in strategic level positions with little or no education and formal training for functioning at the strategic level!

LEVELS OF LEADERSHIP

Leadership, like planning exists on several levels. An accepted model within the US Army categorizes leadership at three primary levels; Strategic; Organizational; and Direct. Review the diagram on page 100. Strategic leadership has a global or national perspective and focuses on improvements and building the organization. Strategic leader's key tenets include the organization's culture, values and purpose. Organizational leadership has an organizational, systems and process perspective and focuses on operating and maintaining the organization. Organizational leader's key tenets include climate, policies and organizational direction. Direct leadership has an individual and small group, task oriented perspective and focuses on influencing and interpersonal realms of the organization. Direct leader's key tenets include cohesion, procedures and motivation. All three levels of leadership are important, yet each serves the organization in different ways from diverse tangents.

Ensuring the members selected for your planning team can think at the strategic level by removing themselves from their day-to-day frame of reference will expedite the plan-building process. Selecting members who think about issues differently will create your strongest team. Teams that have been formed by selecting members from every level of the organization (top-to-bottom level) can become mired in protracted discussions and war-stories about experiences and activities at the operational and tactical levels.

FOUR

Building the Organizational Future Together – How To Get Started!

The Building Blocks

After you have a team selected and you are sure you have the right people, you are ready to get them together and start the 'forming,' 'storming' and 'norming' process of group dynamics. Let's talk about some of the things to consider as you approach this team process. How do things like meeting location, meeting rules and group dynamics affect your efforts? Should this process be facilitated — if so by whom? Even small details like 'what to wear' can have an impact on the openness and candor of your discussions.

Location, Location, Location

Where do you conduct this team process? I recommend you select a location away from your organizational identity. By that I mean both location and nexus. Don't use a conference room in one of your customer's buildings just because it is convenient and available to you at no cost. Remove your team from all organizational linkage to the greatest extent possible. Get away to a distant location where minds can begin to open up and the reminders of clients, stresses and pending contracts can be distant. Choose a relaxing resort or getaway location that lends itself to conducting team business with an enjoyable setting for evening social activities — which leverage team building. Provide privacy and separation for attendees with collective dining opportunities. A terrific amount of follow-on chatter will take place about working-session discussions. Encourage this exchange by creating a casual and informal setting for your team.

I recently read another author's perspective on these kind of team-oriented retreats. He was critical of these displaced team sessions as he suggested it was all about the break from traditional working environments. Using a getaway location is all about creating an environment conducive to creative thinking. Its all about thinking outside of routine constraints, outside of routine ways and about the organization's future outside of routine expectations.

Provide ample advance written instructions for your working sessions. Remember, attendees worried about car parking or restaurant reservations only have their mind half involved with the discussion at hand. Specify business-casual attire and preplan lunches to be semi-working lunches. Nothing halts the discussion momentum faster than the psychological intervention of a 90 minute lunch diversion. Lunches conducted in the same room keep the group focused on the group's notes posted on walls and on earlier discussions, yet provide an opportunity to chat with different table-mates. It's good to keep everyone focused while allowing for some relaxation and brain-breaks.

In all aspects you should be trying to de-emphasize the difference in team member's positions. When the 'boss' is present group *dynamics* can become *static* or 'un-dynamic.' Before the meeting ask the 'boss' to hold his or her specific opinions until others have spoken on a topic, then offering their insights or thoughts as an observation. Once the boss says, "a good idea might be to . . ." the free flowing ideas halt quickly. Ask one of the most senior leaders present to remind the group everyone's opinion will make the ultimate product better. Lower ranking team members may quietly withdraw from some discussions if not encouraged a little by leaders.

CAN WE DO IT OURSELVES?

Hire a qualified strategic planning facilitator to orchestrate your actual meetings. There are many facilitators available so speak with several. Chose a facilitator well in advance so pre-meetings can be accomplished with the CEO and the project manager. It's key for this facilitator to be trained and experienced with **strategic planning specifically**. Using in-house employees just because they have lead group discussions previously will fall far short of your best product—trust me! An excellent facilitator will get familiar with the core aspects of your business, will know your organizational jargon and will know almost everyone's name. You need the objectivity and professional candor of a third party facilitator to keep everyone on an equal playing field. Keep in mind, you are building what may be the most significant pivotal point your organization has approached, do you really want to have this process coached by someone with minimal experience?

HOW LONG SHOULD IT TAKE?

Based on my experience facilitating numerous senior leadership teams, an inaugural strategic plan, for a small to medium sized organization, will require 6-10 sessions (see References & Resources for definition). This varies somewhat depending upon several things:

- Experience and planning knowledge of the team members.

- Does the organization already have validated Values, and a Vision and Mission?
- Willingness of organizational leadership to be open and honest in their discussions.
- Level of enthusiasm of participants and setting.
- Level of ambition for organizational growth.
- Senior leadership being fully committed participants.
- Senior leader's full attendance.
- Discipline of attendees during each session

WHAT ABOUT THE BOSS?

The degree of participation and dedication to the strategic planning process by the President, CEO, COO, etc., is directly proportional to the positive impact your strategic plan will have on the organization. Plain and simple, the influence the boss can cascade over your deployment phase and execution phase will have exponential impact on your strategic plan's effectiveness.

One of the greatest challenges inherent to this process is employee buy-in. I describe in chapter 6, in the deployment phase, these particulars but you should know the personal involvement of the senior leader will make or break most strategic plans. Remember, this is a strategic plan, not an *operational* or *tactical* plan—exactly what the boss's previous experience was in planning may, or may not provide a sound experience for a strategic plan. This time it is different. If there is ever a time for an organization to have a senior cheerleader—this is it! The *commander's intent*, the CEO's intentions, must be heard and understood by every planning team member. He or she must demonstrate the importance of this strategic plan by attending every meeting, personally leading the charge during the employee deployment phase and by steadfast support during the execution phase.

Five

RESOURCE LINKS

LINK TO YOUR RESOURCING PROCESS

The lifeblood of any organization has always been and probably remains the resource trail. It doesn't matter what type of organizational structure you are part of, be it governmental, private sector, 501 (c) (3), military or education. If you follow the resource or budgetary trail from the headwaters of corporate sales, congressional appropriation, donations or grants you will get at what is truly important within an organization's context. Everyone has heard and understands, *only those things that get resourced, actually get accomplished*. It's a reasonable presumption and expectation that eludes many a CEO and Board of Directors.

Why are we surprised when we don't accomplish those things we said were important during last year's Executive Retreat? Those Goals and Objectives sounded great! Everyone agreed they were the right things to proceed with. You made a big splash about them at the annual stockholders meeting and the employee 'Town Hall' get-together. What happened? What didn't happen? How did it fail to happen?

25

Linking strategic Goals and Objectives with the organizational resourcing process is a *mandatory bridge* critical to a successful strategic planning process, albeit one of the most absent elements of strategic plans. In fact, CEOs can be tough to convince that strategic planning can accomplish their real agendas, because so many have tried strategic planning and failed with it miserably — often because no resourcing linkage was formally constructed. A key element to institutionalize with your Strategic Planning Team is this formal connection with your specific organizational resourcing process. Sure, every organization's resourcing process is slightly different — that's OK. Whatever style of budgetary process your organization uses, create a recurring connection that causes your strategic Objectives to be financially assessed every month. Linking to this process and keeping it foremost in the minds and actions of senior leaders is paramount to maintaining the vitality of your Strategic Plan.

CYCLIC RESOURCE REVIEWS

Military organizations manage their financial resources by senior level committees known as Program Budget Advisory Committees (PBACs). Top performing military organizations conduct such meetings monthly to keep these vast budgets in compliance with a multitude of government regulations, statutes and congressional mandates. Universities may use a similar committee process for similar reasons. Private sector enterprises have myriad methodologies for managing their resources ranging from lock-step processes minutely defined to 'hip-pocket' approaches still surviving in very small businesses.

Conducting monthly budget meetings or reviews, of the budget execution process, presents a best-case opportunity for ensuring strategic Objectives are being adequately resourced. Senior resource managers must re-address the strategic plan Goals and Objectives in a deliberate methodical process each month. Discussions must validate accurate resourcing actions were initiated and are keeping pace with execution actions required to accomplish every strategic Objective. Often times, well-intended Action Plans require more resourcing, or resourcing adjustments as progress is made towards strategic Objective accomplishments. Unknown budget requirements upset the process and cause us to re-set our initial resource plans or allocations. Budget management on a lesser frequency may not allow for timely resource reactions or management, critical to Objective accomplishment. Remember your strategic plan must be responsive to ever-changing strategic environments. The realities of a world marketplace influence us in much greater ways than we like to acknowledge. When you think about the fluctuations in the prices of critical commodities, transportation and environmental impacts, it just makes sense to ensure you can react financially to the changing needs in accomplishing strategic objectives.

DELIBERATE DISCUSSIONS — VALIDATING THE RESOURCE LINKS

A great way to ensure there are no unknown hurdles in accomplishing your Action Plans is to require each and every Strategic Objective be discussed during every budget meeting. What do the respective Strategic Objective *metrics* tell you? Are there resource impediments occurring that were unforeseen? Do resource excesses exist where you are under-spending your Action Plans? Have you realized cost savings or cost avoidances you didn't expect? Can you shift such resource excesses to other strategic Objective Action Plans?

A second-order benefit to reviewing each strategic Objective during every budget meeting, is the organizational alignment and synergy created by the group discussion. Bear in mind, not every resource manager has 'bought into' your strategic planning process with the same gusto. Recurring discussions about resourcing each strategic Objective help to clarify priorities, revalidate organizational direction and underscore the organization's Vision and Mission. Third-order benefits like keeping *all* senior leaders focused on the established priorities expand the organizational alignment footprint throughout the ranks. It is essential to circle-back to the Strategic Plan at most meetings, certainly budget meetings, to remind corporate energies where you are heading, why it is important and how you will accomplish established Action Plans.

As work-teams execute their unique Action Plans in support of accomplishing strategic Objectives, remember their resource requirements change in several ways. Each work-team's resource needs are different and these differences are reflected in their budget estimates. Keeping previous budget forecasts linked to actual budget execution, remains critically important. Second, work-team's resource requirements ebb or surge during different times throughout the budget cycle, as compared to other work-teams. Monthly budget reviews, through the perspective of each Strategic Objective, force you to consider these differences. Mission-creep and sloppy budget execution within pockets of the organization can cause broad-scale tilts, eroding overall team success across the organizational spectrum.

PROOFING THE PROCESS USING RESOURCE PRIORITIES

In large organizations, especially horizontal organizations, it is easy for functional area-specific Directors, regional Vice Presidents or geographically separated elements to pay more attention to their own 'local' agendas. Resource priorities at the 'small end of the whip' don't always reflect the greater organizational direction, although they should. Senior leaders can monitor organizational alignment and unity-of-effort by using resource management as a tool for 'proofing.' Do your monthly expenditure reports reflect the priorities established for strategic Objectives?

PAINTING THE PICTURE — EDUCATING THE TEAM

Make a deliberate effort in your Strategic Plan to graphically portray your resource management process and illustrate how this process is linked to your Strategic Plan. Now every stakeholder, ideally every member of the organization can understand how the 'ends,' 'ways' and 'means' are connected. Informed and knowledgeable team members are the best insurance in accomplishing strategic Goals and Objectives. At your annual Strategic Planning 'Off-Site Review,' ensure a comprehensive review of the organizational budget. How did your budget estimates and forecasts compare to actual execution? Were your resource projections accurate and did you adjust financial execution actions as actual financial requirements changed during the budget cycle? Were essential strategic objectives ignored by pockets of the organization as indicated by resource execution? Making resource or budget reviews part of your Strategic Planning review cycle will ensure these critical organizational elements are inextricably linked.

SIX

THE STRATEGIC PLANNING PROCESS

Think about strategic planning as a process consisting of three key Phases. They look like this:

- *Preparing the organization* for strategic planning and selecting your planning team.

- Actually *building your Strategic Plan* including the resource management links, the annual review cycle/process, designing meaningful metrics for monitoring each strategic Objective and ultimately deploying your plan to team members, stakeholders and customers.

- *Reviewing and updating your Strategic Plan* and making annual adjustments.

IS EVERYONE READY FOR THIS?

Strategic planning for many organizations remains a mysterious process. It may be time to add a strategic dimension to your organization for any number of reasons: continued growth or instability created by growth; proactive movement towards quality initiatives; international certification of your organization, such as the various ISO protocols, may demand you stabilize and codify your planning process beyond the operational planning you have already been doing. Let's acknowledge, strategic planning presupposes a higher level of management sophistication. Strategic planning is only found in organizations that are driving for their fullest potential. No matter your reasons, embarking on this process does require some preparation of your senior leaders and your total workforce in general.

Announcing your strategic planning intentions and selecting a planning team will signify to some change in the organizational *climate* is forthcoming. Sound strategic planning is much more comprehensive than just creating a climate change. Astute leaders will recognize this initiative as an opportunity to improve or transition the organizational *culture*—a far more permanent, leading change that can mould the organization's future. This is a key time for the CEO to lead the charge. Being a transformational leader, the real 'change manager' for the organization, is a key unwritten responsibility of every CEO. Even the initial announcement of your intentions to conduct strategic planning is important to the eventual planning process. You already know how important first impressions are, it also applies here. Clear delineations between this planning process and previous *climate* changes (flavors of the month) are essential. This is not an announcement that should be delegated to senior Vice Presidents or other juniors—this is the time for the *Boss* to assert her or his intent and set the stage for proactive change. As myriad authors remind us, an organization is either changing or dying!

Your initial announcement might be to the most senior leaders in private—a clear warning real change is necessary, inevitable and the proper course for the organization. Cascading messages should be delivered to all middle managers to clarify this exciting initiative, helping *sup porting* team members to better understand their essential roles in this transformation. Why the repeated reference to transformation—because transformation will be the actual result of a properly developed and executed strategic planning process. Proactive change—a *vast improvement* in your organization will occur exponentially. I am not suggesting incidental improvements, rather much greater improvements than your history might reveal. Strategic planning will ratchet organizational performance beyond levels thought possible, when done correctly and when lead with great enthusiasm.

Are your senior leaders really ready for this? I can tell you, your planning team will experience more than one embarrassing moment as you work through this comprehensive process. It is the right time for some deep introspective review. Strategic planning is a process that will illuminate things previously overlooked that should not have been overlooked. It is a process that will highlight good-ole-boy tendencies and clarify the tough choices driven by your future. While working with your planning team, dissecting the strengths and weaknesses of your organization, more than once planning team members will sit back and smile as a wave of 'committee guilt' washes over their past decisions and well-intended efforts. Don't be stymied or put off by these truisms, trust me, each of these things will happen—and it's OK—in fact it may be the greatest team building exercise your senior leaders ever experience. Relax with it and discuss the rough spots during evening social events, nothing here to be ashamed of. Remember, the fact you and your senior leaders are willing to take such an in-depth diagnostic look at your organization will create huge new benefits, opportunities for both organizational and personal growth. It can be both very exciting and somewhat uncomfortable at times.

BUILDING A STRATEGIC PLAN –
11 STEPS TO ACHIEVE YOUR VISION

There are 11 basic Steps in the development of a comprehensive strategic plan. Numerous authors compress or expand this process but I believe 11 steps best defines the process. It's essential to pursue these 11 steps in the correct sequence. Depending on the *planning experience* and the cohesion of your planning team, many of these steps can be con-joined during planning team meetings. You must understand taking shortcuts or attempting to homogenize these 11 steps into something fewer will have an adverse affect on your final strategic planning product. I have watched organizations, even facilitators, compress these steps into finite 'time boxes,' setting aside only so much time for each step. Don't be tempted to rush the process in this way. One or two meetings saved becomes a 'penny wise and dollar foolish' compromise—like buying the cheapest motorcycle helmet—why would anyone be so near-sighted! Take the time necessary to accomplish this process, in the sequence I present it.

There are a 100 ways to build a strategic plan—most of them are not completely wrong by any empirical standard—yet each produces a slightly different planning product. Make this investment of time, albeit very expensive senior leader time, a worthwhile opportunity to map out your organization's future. This plan will become how you achieve your organizational Vision. This plan may become the most influential *culture-changing* instrument ever applied to your organization—don't be tempted to compromise it by trying to save a three day off-site meeting, or a few day-long discussions just because of operational pressures. Stay the course and work through these 11 Steps, you will thank yourself many times over.

I. Information Gathering—the Environmental Scan

Gather all of the organizational plans that remain completely or partially in effect. The organizational Long Range Plan (a 5-20 year outlook), quality initiative implementation plans, marketing plans and sales plans or forecasts. Collect valid industry trends, professional articles from trade journals, take-home packets from all of the conferences your key leaders have attended in the past two years. You know the ones I'm referring to, the product development trade fairs, the annual industry products trade shows, the new automation program meeting that your IT guys just attended, etc.

Pile up the plans you have received from your higher-echelon corporate holding company that have impact of your organization's future or flexibility. Pull out those customer survey results and employee survey results no one wanted to believe at last year's executive retreat. Now is the time to review them all in greater detail, gleaning out *the impacts* on the organization that may have been dismissed or overlooked before. Possibly the timing of operational issues now changes potential impacts previously set aside.

It is time to analyze these things that may have not received your full attention previously. This time-consuming analytic process is a great staff development opportunity. I encourage clients to assign this analysis to their second and third tier managers. Use the 'fast trackers,' the up-and-comers that demonstrate ambition and innovative thinking. Task this group of go-getters to scrutinize every detail of these reports and plans with an eye to *how do these things impact our organization?*

At the same time ask this talent pool to list a few counter-measures, ways that these adverse or potentially adverse impacts can be spun or leveraged and turned into an advantage or opportunity. Have each analyst prepare a brief one page synopsis for each report, plan or conference bring-home packet. This analysis may take several weeks but it is important leg-work to have accomplished before you start your strategic planning team efforts. It is also a great way to start to imbed strategic thinking into the operational managers who will someday be the strategic leaders of your organization.

Circulate these new impact-briefs, as a read-ahead packet, throughout the Strategic Planning Team several weeks before your first meeting. Ensure these are read and understood by every planning team member and consider leading a group discussion about them before you formally launch into your strategic planning sessions. Time spent here understanding the potential and real impacts of new markets, technologies, competitors and emerging regulatory constraints will speed and improve your formal planning sessions in the weeks to follow. Accomplished by junior leaders and discussed within a strategic context, the Environmental Scan Step can be a huge macro-team building process, the initial movement of *organizational alignment.*

II. BUILDING THE VISION, MISSION AND VALUES – AND A FEW PLANNING ASSUMPTIONS

It's time to meet with your Strategic Planning Team and formally start your strategic planning journey. The value and perceived importance of this first team meeting cannot be overstated. It will simply be exactly what you make it to be — nothing more, nothing less. It doesn't hurt to open such a first meeting with a futurist's video. Several futurists like Joel Barker or Dewitt Jones have produced numerous videos and all provoke proactive thought and set a stage for futuristic or visionary thinking — a good context in which to make your transformation comments. Think high-energy, motivation and bold leadership — grab the attentions of this great talent pool and charge into your future. This is a great *leading* opportunity for the CEO to assert themselves as the change manager and founder of this all-important initiative.

Depending whether yours is a private sector enterprise, public sector, possibly even a military organization, the sequence for Vision, Mission and Values may vary (or Mission, Vision and Values for the military) (or Values, Vision and Mission for a religious organization). It doesn't really matter the Vision-Mission-Values sequence in so long as you clarify it and make sense of it for your particular organization. Most organizations will place the Vision first, it paints the picture of a future end-state you are striving to achieve. Followed by the Mission second, which will clarify specifically what it is your organization actually does. Finally, the Values should define the desired organizational tenets and behaviors, using examples of expected corporate *and* personal behaviors. Stating clearly the desired demonstrated behaviors is essential for everyone in your organization to easily understand your Values. For example, consider the value Integrity. What does this value actually look like when we demonstrate it in the workplace?

Michigan's dynamic Governor Jennifer Granholm tells her 50,000+ state employees that integrity in the workplace means "we do what we say and we say what we do." This is just a example of her proactive Visions and Values Workshop initiative, deployed face-to-face to every State of Michigan employee by trained facilitators. This initiative created an opportunity to improve the morale, integrity and motivation of a civil service workforce hungering for leadership, support and the backing of senior leaders.

It is very important to have your planning team work through these discussions as a group. I like to use large pads of plain paper on standing easels to capture the group's phraseology and subsequent word-smithing. Yes, it takes time. A lot more time than anyone ever believes it might—that's OK! Take the time, encourage the discussion, the ensuing word-smithing and all of the contributory thoughts everyone will have for why a certain word makes it 'just right.' Sure one can use a computer and projector and electronically write/re-write the group's words, but there are a few disadvantages to this electronic medium. There is some value in allowing the group to see crossed-out words, lined-through phrases and changes to syntax. Posting these large sheets of paper on the meeting room walls also provokes additional thoughts—something a computer can't do.

This is team-building, group bonding and transformative synergy at its best. It is also a basis for organizational alignment, your senior leaders are starting to agree, or at least come to consensus about key cornerstones of the organization. Even the foot draggers and nay-sayers will take an active part in getting their thoughts and ideas into the discussion—exactly the group dynamics you wanted! While it may be comfortable to believe everyone already has the same beliefs, ideas and thoughts about the organization's future, this process of co-authorship, actually group authorship, codifies consensus among your team.

Vision

There are a few simple rules to follow that ensure your finished **Vision** will serve you well in practice and in efforts to align the organization. Let's look at a few:

VISION

- Should paint a picture of where your organization wants to go.

- Is focused on the future, but still achievable.

- Captures the reader's heart and inspires one towards this organization's desired end-state.

- Should be enduring, not changing very often or never substantially.

- Should motivate the reader in a figurative direction.

- Key words or feelings; inspiring, motivational, enduring, realistic, clear in intent, believable.

When you complete your consensus-agreed upon Vision, post it on the wall for reference during your Mission and Values discussions. It's surprising how often you will go back and re-read, or modify what you have already set 'in clay'(Another advantage to a low-tech approach for this process.). Ideally your Vision will be inspiring, closing your eyes and hearing it should instill what the future looks like, maybe a better place or engendering higher organizational performance. It should set your organization apart from any other—even those others in the same industry or with a similar purpose.

Mission

For most organizations, the Mission will be your second element to build. If your Vision is considered your first element, then your Mission should clarify to all exactly what your organization actually does, not what it *hopes to do*, or what it *used to do*, rather what your organization actually does, specifically. It should define or clarify your organizational role and purpose—for anyone, not just those that are already familiar with your organization.

Again, your strategic planning team must work through this discussion as a group. Like the Vision building segment, it takes time. It takes patience. It requires lots of examples by team members, numerous war-stories and plenty of rehashing. Again, that's OK! A good facilitator will help guide you through this and keep the group focused. Sticking with the group's rules you agreed upon at the beginning of your meeting and having an objective 'third party' facilitator keeping things moving will serve you well. In my experience it is not unusual for a group to consume a half-day just getting the Vision and Mission built. This may seem lengthy at first, but believe me, the discussions and word-smithing are valuable and worthwhile efforts in the overall process. You are laying a foundation with these key elements, a foundation you will rely on to project your movement to the future *from*. It is putzy, painstaking work, but valuable side benefits are generated.

In building your Mission statement answer, the unasked question—is simply, why do we exist? There are a few simple rules to follow that ensure your finished **Mission** statement will serve you well in execution and in efforts to align the organization. Let's look at a few:

MISSION

- Concise sentences which are clear and easy to understand.
- Related to attracting and retaining resources.
- Reasonably enduring, stable for several years.
- Related to a realistic capability of the organization.
- Major functions performed in order to accomplish your Mission.

A well written Mission statement will answer the basic **What**, for **Whom** and **How** will we perform this and also **Why** we exist or produce this product/service. In military organizations and certain public sector organizations such as police, fire or public utilities, the Mission statement may precede the Vision statement because the Mission may be dictated by statute or higher authority. In these cases, the Vision then follows as the second element and becomes an *interpretive catalyst* for executing the dictated Mission.

Values

Your organizational Values should be discussed and word-smithed through in a similar fashion as the Vision statement and Mission statement for all of the same reasons. Co-authorship will ensure consensus and durability for all to abide by. I have watched a few CEOs dictate the Values for their organization with a resultant passé acceptance by some senior leaders and most juniors. Will such Values really influence personal and organizational behaviors? It remains incredibly important for everyone on the strategic planning team to have the chance to ante-in their thoughts, beliefs and reasons-why. In this developmental phase of building your strategic plan, maintaining team unity and creating team buy-in is essential.

Values are difficult for most people to identify because we confuse ourselves with ideals or desirable actions. For example, *working together* is not a value, rather identify teamwork. *Diversity* is not a value, better to identify inclusion. *Good management* is unspecific, rather identify leadership. *Accountability* is too general, rather identify integrity. Your group discussions will develop associated terms that can be combined or grouped and better stated with a different word. Keep your organizational list of Values to 5-8 at most, fewer is always better. Building a representative acronym may help people to recognize and relate to your bedrock Values.

The essential rule to follow when establishing Values is to define the *demonstrated behaviors* that portray each Value. We would all agree integrity is a great Value—but what does it look like in the workplace? I think I have it, but how will others see and know I am applying integrity to my organizational actions? Ask your planning team to coin a phrase that typifies what integrity looks like. For example, your team selects Honesty as a Value. Defining it as "tell the boss the full and complete issue, focusing on the fix, not the fault," may be more meaningful and engender the kind of honest behaviors you want the rank and file team members to actually demonstrate in their daily actions. Focusing on the desired demonstrated behaviors will clarify what 'right' looks like. Remember the old telephone game, passing a message around a circle of colleagues to demonstrate communications skills? Each of us well intended souls has our own perception of what 'right' looks like—make it crystal clear what 'right' looks like for *your* organization.

Word-smithing Values with a group of 15 senior leaders can take a large portion of a day. You can shorten this important process by providing 40-50 Values, each on separate index cards, to each table group. As each small-group selects their most meaningful Values and then presents them to the whole group, a common group of Values will emerge and be agreed upon within a few hours. Discussion, group consensus and group decision, all achieved in a more streamlined way. In this way you have maintained an open forum for discussion and crafted co-authorship.

III. PLANNING ASSUMPTIONS

After you've completed building your Vision, Mission and Values it's a good time to reach planning team consensus about some basic planning assumptions. Establishing these as a presumption or 'given' will spare the team consternation and dozens of 'what if' stories that naturally arise during the next several meetings. After thoroughly discussing the staff analysis products from Step I, the scan of your organizational environment — capture a list of planning assumptions that may remain constant for the immediate two-three years. Basic market trends, demographic trends, employment probabilities, etc. Assume things that apply to your organization and your immediate future, e.g., statutes limiting foreign ownership of certain technologies will remain in place; demographic downtrends for this geographic area will continue; unemployment will stay at 10% or more in your metropolitan area; etc. By listing these for the planning team and posting them on the wall while you conduct your planning sessions, you will remove some of the 'exceptions and clutter' that constrain creative thoughts. Talking about these issues will also open some team member's minds to thinking about longer-term issues and bigger-picture issues than they may be accustomed to thinking about.

Remember, you are trying to pull team member's thoughts out of their usual *operational realms* and get them thinking about **strategic issues** and **strategic timeframes**. This level of thinking is not instinctual, it is hard for many of us to move into the strategic realm.

What do you do with planning assumptions after you have completed your strategic plan? Use them as points of reference and examples as you deploy your strategic plan to all organizational employees. Remembering your planning team discussions and citing these as examples later will keep them in the minds of all employees and remind everyone of the complexities and variables considered during your strategic planning process.

IV.   ORGANIZATIONAL STRENGTHS, WEAKNESSES, OPPORTUNITIES AND THREATS (SWOT)

Determining **where you are** is essential before beginning any journey, this truism remains appropriate for strategic planning. As you conduct your SWOT analysis you'll be surprised at how much you learn about your organization. Many things will take on greater meaning and the connection between various aspects of your organizational future will begin to become clear. Every good MBA program will tell you the Strengths and Weaknesses you discuss and record are 'internal' elements of your organizational location—**where you are today**. Likewise, the Opportunities and Threats are said to be 'external' to your organization—elements of the strategic environment in which your organization operates. I agree with this assessment mostly but I will offer an additional thought to consider on this internal/external perspective.

Many of these strengths and weaknesses will be the very capabilities and technological specialties from which your organization was built from. Others will be by-products of the leadership climate or organizational culture. When discussing your Opportunities and Threats, remember to include those things that teeter between a Weakness and a Threat, or a Strength and an Opportunity. For example, your team openly discusses the corporate tendency to promote only from within—is this truly a weakness, or is it more a strength or maybe even a threat? I'm not sure—a lot depends on the results, not only of such actions but of the second-order affects of such actions. Have these been staff promotions that killed the infusion of fresh ideas and newer schools-of-thought outsiders may have brought in?

I recommend you record all of your SWOT elements in large letters on large sheets of paper and tape them up around the room as you work. Yes, I know a low-tech method, but quite effective! You will go back to previous elements over and over again. This also provides a visual stimulus for more creative thoughts, thought provocation and simple reminders for team members that will spare you numerous questions. When capturing your SWOT elements, use an additional person as a recorder in addition to your facilitator. Advise your recorder not to enter into this discussion process—simply have your recorder write legibly and keep pace with the group discussion.

SWOT discussions are fast moving and exciting, a good facilitator will keep things moving and provide directions to the recorder simultaneously. These discussions are not quite as wide open as true brainstorming (where everything is captured) but most things get captured if there appears to be a quorum of agreement the suggestion is valid. For example, "we build good cars" offered as one of your strengths. Where most team members agree it is true, capture it as a Strength element. A few will offer protest and cite a recent survey that indicates our cars were third in consumer quality ratings, one will comment we don't build them as well as we used to—so on and so forth. It is important not to let the group get off-track and venture down a 'war story' side-track. If there appears a quorum, capture it and the group will reassess it later during the prioritization portion of the process. Keep things moving, keep the discussion focused on the correct grouping (ie., strengths, weaknesses, etc.) A good facilitator will test the planning team by asking for group consensus as questionable elements are cited, "is that really a Strength or maybe a Weakness?"

List and post all of the sheets containing Strengths, Weaknesses, Opportunities and Threats. Label the top of each sheet for easy reference for each element, Strength, Weakness, Threat or Opportunity (SWOT). Now review them all as a group, looping and restating those elements that are nearly identical or so similar as to lose distinction. Whittle these four lists down to maybe 10-15 elements for each SWOT category.

Expect the list of weaknesses will always be the short-est—that's OK. It's human nature not to address our weak-nesses as quick as other aspects. Yes, I know the list of strengths will be built the quickest—we are quick to clarify those things we think we are good at.

Now ask your planning team to look back through each of the four categories and as a group **prioritize every cap-tured entry** by writing a number 1, 2, 3, 4 or 5 beside it. Weigh every entry by *the size of the impact it has or may have on the organization.* This is done simply for relativity. Planning team members must understand as you use these SWOT el-ement-listings, not every element has equal value because of the difference in impact on the organization. It is good to stay aware of them all, yet equal consideration cannot be given to each item listed. A good facilitator and recorder can shepherd your planning team through this SWOT process in one day. That might sound lengthy to you, but there is a great deal of discussion and milling-out with most every captured entry. It's important to have these discussions and build your SWOT listings completely. You will see the planning team synergy building throughout this process.

Allow me to share a simple caution, a reminder for this part of the process. The group's most senior leader, by position, will harvest the greatest planning team efforts by opining less and listening more during your SWOT process. If the CEO, president or whoever your most senior leader is, speaks towards the end of each compartmented discussion, greater objectivity and sharing will occur. In the military we label these opinions sarcastically as 'GOBIs,' that is a General Officer Bright Idea. Most generals understand such phenomena and wait to hear juniors sharing their insights first. Sometimes the senior leader speaks too early, of course then juniors quickly line up to agree with the boss and little objective sharing occurs. A good facilitator will monitor this and adjust such sequencing by discreet side-bar coaching.

V. ALTERNATIVE FUTURES – AND THE FUTURE

It's time for some out-of-the-box creativity. It is incredibly important for your planning team to explore what the organizational future might look like – and what it *will* look like as based on the analysis and the *location-finding* accomplished so far. Most organizations have not done this. Futures are often the personal opinions of only the most senior leaders, sometimes shared, sometimes not – almost always based upon nothing more scientific than 'I think' premises. You have already completed dozens of staff papers summarizing a comprehensive scan of your organizational environment, by various subjects. You have developed a Vision that ought to paint a picture of your desired end-state. Your planning team discussed and listed numerous planning assumptions that form a basis for your strategic planning venue. Your planning team has completed an in-depth, honest and objective assessment of your SWOT—**where your organization is today** and the kind of issues it is facing in the 3-5 year future.

Divide your strategic planning team into two groups. Segregate these groups for two hours and ask each group to compose a synopsis of what they believe the future looks like for your organization—at the end of 5 years. Bring the two groups back together and ask each group to present their future synopsis and explain the basis for it—using the environmental scan summaries, planning assumptions, Vision and SWOT listings. I expect you will find these two alternative futures to be 80+% similar, as one might expect given the same background materials. After a thorough 'murder board' discussion of each group's alternative future, facilitate a large group composition of 'The Future,' as envisioned by large group consensus.

I want to state another procedural caution here. Keep these developmental products secure within the strategic planning team. It would be premature and unfortunate if your organizational future cites *a 20% reduction in the workforce within 3 years* and then have this revelation shared with employees outside of the planning context that created such discussions. Your strategic planning team discussions should include disclosure sensitivities when you first meet with them. Reach group consensus about planning team rules and ensure everyone understands the implications of these issues.

VI.   FIXING THE GAPS – BUILDING STRATEGIC OBJECTIVES AND STRATEGIES

First it is essential to understand the relationship between strategic Goals, Objectives and Strategies before we explore the process for building them. These strategic planning terms are used incorrectly by many and most often used without understanding the dependent relationship each has upon the others.

Strategic Goals are general in nature and encompass broad subject areas that are important for the organization to reach its Vision. Strategic Goals are stated in short, concise terms, usually only a few words. Goals are not specific enough to be measured separately, rather the accomplishment of the Goal is only realized upon the accomplishment of each and all supporting strategic Objectives. A strategic Goal will include one or several supporting strategic Objectives. Likewise a strategic Objective will usually have one or more specific strategies specified for accomplishment.

A strategic Objective is a specific supplemental element of a strategic Goal **that is absolutely necessary** to achieving that strategic Goal. A strategic Objective is written purposefully using a five point criteria, these are often referenced by the acronym **SMART:**

STRATEGIC OBJECTIVES
▪ Specific
▪ Measurable
▪ Achievable
▪ Results-oriented
▪ Time specific

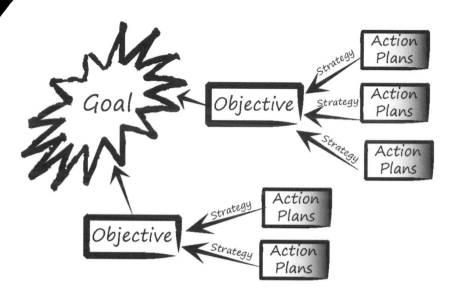

Strategies represent *the way* we intend to achieve a specific strategic Objective. Strategies align the efforts and focus the resources in a priority direction, or upon a specific focal point. The purpose of a strategy is to reduce duplication, eliminate wasted efforts and the counter-productive actions of well intended people trying to accomplish a strategic Objective. Strategies are prescriptive in nature, not merely suggestive.

STRATEGIC GOALS CREATED FROM BRIDGE STATEMENTS

Building strategic Goals is a reasonably straight-forward process. Start by reviewing the Vision, the SWOT category listings and your Future Statement. You know where the organization is, along its timeline progressing towards the Vision. As a planning team, collectively develop a list of 'bridge statements' that would nullify threats, maintain strengths, reduce or eliminate weaknesses and leverage op-portunities to your best advantage. Bear in mind, you may want to discuss how your organization might also transi-tion threats into opportunities. Likewise you always want to deflect or defer threats as much as possible to minimize inevitable impacts on the organization. This is a gap analysis process.

Simply write stand-alone statements that would be necessary to move the organization 'from where it is now, to (or towards) the organization's Vision.' Well written statements can be as simple as "Upgrade the Information Technology department to leverage emerging software for administration and finance."; "Expand sales territories into the Western region."; "Reduce ground-based shipping expenses by 5% each year for 3 years."

Once you have completed developing your 'bridge statements' review them collectively and ensure planning team consensus. Grouping these by general subject is next. It is not necessary these various 'bridge statements' have a direct nexus or a cascade relationship with one another. Simply group them by general theme. Using obvious themes creates enough correlation for the purpose of building strategic Goals. Clearly written bridge-statement commonalities will produce groups such as: improving the workplace environment; increasing product sales; improving employee trust, understanding and teamwork, etc.

This grouping process can be accomplished by any one of several affinity exercise methods. I have had only limited success *looping and grouping* the 'bridge statements,' as listed on posted sheets of large paper, with the planning team collectively. A much better method I think is to place each 'bridge statement' on a separate index card. Place all of these 'bridge statement' cards on a table and ask the planning team to arrange them into groups by general theme. Each person will move them around according to their own thoughts, each person's arrangement provoking another's new arrangement. Encourage all team members to continuously circle the table while discussing the card's statements. Within 30 minutes most planning teams will have reached a settling point — now you've reached group consensus with less story-telling and fewer side-track examples. Getting team members up and walking around a large table ensures every team member is active in this process. Other methods are not as favorable as it allows shy team members to be silent while the facilitator, with only a few vocal team members control the process. Any affinity process can work, but it is critical each theme-group contains only one theme, no more.

After creating these new theme-groups, simply craft a short general statement that captures the grouping's theme — a new strategic Goal! Ideally you will create 4-8 strategic Goals. There is nothing magic about these numbers, although fewer than four Goals suggests groupings that are too broad and more than eight Goals suggests theme statements that may be too specific.

CRAFTING STRATEGIC OBJECTIVES — IN A **SMART** WAY

OK, now you have a list of strategic Goals. Hopefully you have created at least four and not more than 7-8 Goals. At this point these Goals are randomly listed. Group consensus can affix numbers to them later based upon a logical sequence for presentation. Developing the supporting strategic Objectives is the most difficult aspect of strategic planning. Yet, it represents the heart of strategic plans — the very essence of What you are trying to achieve.

By their very definition, strategic Objectives are a *critical imperative* to achieving a strategic Goal. Strategic Objectives should be completed in 1-3 years, no longer. In other words, every strategic Objective must be accomplished for the strategic Goal to be achieved. If most, but not all Objectives are achieved, the strategic Goal remains incomplete. Every strategic Objective is essential to Goal achievement.

Earlier I highlighted the elements of every correctly

written strategic Objective, the *SMART* criteria. The criticality of these elements cannot be understated. One of the more common faults of Strategic Plans are poorly written strategic Objectives. Many Strategic Plans fail to achieve their stated Goals due to poorly designed (written) strategic Objectives. The underlying rationale is, "if you can't measure it, you can't manage it" — of course if you are not measuring strategic Objective progress you will never know when, or if, such Objectives are achieved.

All groups muddle through this group-writing process at first, then after a few painfully slow-build Objectives are written, the pace quickens and your team speeds through the remainder.

Let me make a strong suggestion for this critical creative step. A complete Strategic Plan should have 20 or fewer strategic Objectives. Again, nothing magic about this number, however organizations with greater than 20 strategic Objectives find it exponentially difficult to achieve success in their Strategic Plan execution. Fewer is always better during this process. Fewer Goals are better than more. Fewer Objectives are better than more. Fewer strategies are better than more…and so on.

Group patience will dictate the best technology for developing strategic Objectives — either whiteboard or computer/projector. Either can be very effective, each with its own advantages and disadvantages. The great advantage with the low-tech practice is in the physical posting of the large sheets around your room. These group products provoke thought, stimulate shy and quiet members and serve as visual reminders of earlier thoughts and ideas.

I like to assign a few group members to be the stewards for each element of criteria: Specific; Measurable; Achievable; Results-oriented; Time specific. Quickly your group will identify their composition deficiencies and then craft SMART strategic Objectives. Don't cut corners by creating strategic Objectives *almost* SMART. Where you must be Time specific, use month, date and year—not 1st Quarter FY2012. Be specific in all aspects of each strategic Objective. Validate with your group the strategic Objective is really Achievable. Specify the exact Result you are striving for. Don't settle for ambiguous phrases that can be interpreted in several ways.

Every reader should be able to identify the five elements of a SMART strategic Objective. Remember, strategic Objectives need to be crystal clear to every reader, stakeholder and team member—especially those readers outside your specialty domain.

EXAMPLES OF **SMART** OBJECTIVES:

- *"Design, fund and build the Homeland Security Training Center by September 30, 2012"*
- *"Ensure all employees are exposed to the Mission, Vision and Values of the ABC Corporation by October 1, 2011 and understand how their responsibilities support that Vision."*
- *"Directorates will verify, validate and improve core processes and submit flowcharts to the Chief of Staff, by September 15th annually."*
- *"Realign the XYZ Continuous Quality Improvement (CQI) manual and program with Malcolm Baldrige criteria by January 31, 2011."*
- *"All salaried associates must have a valid Personal Development Program (PDP) plan completed annually (updated semiannually) by October 1, 2012."*

Can you identify all five elements of the SMART criteria?

EXAMPLES OF POORLY WORDED OBJECTIVES:

- *"Increase the use of Distance Training Technology (DTT)."*
- *"Attract and retain high quality employees."*
- *"Maintain facilities appearance and operations in the highest state possible."*
- *"Improve vehicle sales to match corporate sales expectations."*
- *"Complete a state-wide Master Plan."*
- *"Implement environmental programs."*
- *"Conduct comprehensive state-wide stakeholder needs analysis."*

What elements of SMART are missing?

STRATEGIES ARE THE ACTIONS FOR SUCCESS!

Strategies tell us *How* you want your organizational team members, employees or associates to approach the accomplishment of strategic Objectives. Strategies are intended to eliminate duplication of effort and minimize the resources required to achieve success. If strategies are not clearly identified in a Strategic Plan, every team member will interpret for themselves the 'best' way to pursue strategic Objectives. Various interpretations lead to redundant efforts, wasting of resources and may delay the accomplishment of strategic Objectives.

Most strategic Objectives will require only one clearly stated Strategy. Occasionally two are needed to clarify a sequential approach towards an Objective. Sometimes the strategic Objective is so simple and straight forward it doesn't require a stated Strategy. As before, fewer Strategies are better. Think of it this way: is there any special guidance we need to provide to assist our organization in achieving this Objective? Is there a special way or unique sequence we want team members or work-teams to pursue? Remember here we want to specify the How element. A direct approach, less susceptible to different interpretations, is best. Strategies are *directive* in nature, *not suggestive*. Team members will learn during your Strategic Plan *deployment process* why you have prescribed specific Strategies. Strategies are intended to assist us with *aligning* the organization, getting all of the various energies of the organization heading in a similar direction. Of course Strategies alone cannot accomplish complete organizational alignment, but they contribute largely to this endeavor.

EXAMPLES OF GOOD STRATEGIES:

- *"Treat this as a priority action for the Chief of Staff and the administrative support team."*
- *"Select partner organizations which offer the greatest advantage to the XYZ Corporation's capabilities."*
- *"Foster an on-going professional relationship with these officials."*
- *"Include this videotape or DVD in presentations."*
- *"Include Economic Impact Report data in presentations."*

EXAMPLES OF POORLY WORDED STRATEGIES:

- *"Improve the implementation process from last year."*
- *"Create more enthusiasm among associates during staff visits."*
- *"Reduce waste and spoilage wherever possible."*

VII. Develop Metrics for Strategic Objectives

Strategic Objectives require a specific metric be developed to actively capture and manage Objective progress. You will recall we earlier defined strategic Goals as being broad brush generalized statements containing a 'theme.' Strategic Objectives are much more specific and measurable, two elements of the SMART criteria we use to write a strategic Objective. Therefore each and every strategic Objective will have a metric associated with it for management purposes.

Metrics generally contain numerous measurements. Simple tracking usually includes only one measurement. Chapter 7 reviews the metrics process in greater detail, here we will only touch on a few basics, enough to acknowledge metrics as an important step in creating a Strategic Plan.

Critical to designing a metric is identifying exactly which elements of the strategic Objective you are going to measure. It is easy to get confused during this process and to ensure best clarity complete the identification process as a group. Everyone 'receives' the written words a little differently. Strategic Objectives written to the SMART criteria reduce this ambiguity a great deal, yet individuals don't always process the same information, exactly the same way.

Analyze this SMART strategic Objective for measuring:

"Identify and secure annual funding, on or before September 30th of each year, for recurring maintenance costs associated with Homeland Security grant-purchased equipment."

As a group, discuss the specific elements of the strategic Objective that will form the basis for metrics measurement. Discussing the strategic Objective's elements of measure with your planning team may seem unnecessary because they were the same group that crafted the strategic

Objective initially, however you will see how important this is as you work through the discussion.

Once you have identified the correct elements necessary to measure it becomes a simple process of completing a spreadsheet style database using an automation program such as Microsoft's Excel. Various macros are commercially available that further simplify this chart-creating process.

After completing a strategic metric for each strategic Objective, collectively build a Target or Success Matrix that portrays all of the strategic Objectives and the targeted date established for completion (see page 125). Creating this matrix as a group will illuminate an obvious chronological order for completion. It is important to understand not every, or even most, strategic Objectives need to be accomplished in the first few years of a Strategic Plan. Remember this is a 3-5 year Strategic Plan. This logical chronological approach to Objective accomplishment increases the probability for success.

VIII. Design a Review Cycle for Your Strategic Plan

Strategic plans must be dynamic and evolving plans. Strategic plans guide us through an ever-changing, evolving strategic environment, hence the planning duration of just 3-5 years. At times, our strategic environment changes significantly over a period of just months. Can anyone deny the world market, macroeconomic or political influences thrust upon our strategic environment in the past three years? Have these changes in the strategic environment impacted your organization? If so, how and to what degree?

To be useful and trusted a Strategic Plan must reflect the realities of the dynamic world around us. Specifically it must reflect those strategic realms that directly link to your organizational operating environment.

A useful and relevant Strategic Plan should be updated every 12-24 months. This updating cycle in no way changes the planning projection period of the Strategic Plan. The effective scope of the Strategic Plan remains 3-5 years. Goals and Objectives that are accomplished can be revised to reflect sustaining desires or removed during your updating process. Target dates for strategic Objective completion may require modification as the strategic environment creates new conditions for your organization. Sometimes Strategies also need to be restated or redirected as efforts illuminate their usefulness and efficiency.

For these and other reasons, a preplanned Review Cycle must be established. The actual process and specific details about how such a review might be accomplished are contained in chapter 10. Make no mistake about it, a preplanned, codified Review Cycle is emblematic of the effectiveness of your Strategic Plan.

IX. Guidance for Action Plans—the Traction Required to Initiate and Sustain Strategic Progress

Action Plans are the working blueprints, the craftsman's drawings that guide team members through strategic progress. Remember, strategic progress at the work-team level of your organization *is in addition to* the normal day-to-day operational and tactical level taskings. These team members do not deliver their skills and ply their talents in the strategic realm, rather they perform operational and tactical assignments and accomplish product production within the operational and tactical levels of your organization.

Work teams must digest and absorb a Strategic Plan and then determine which strategic Objectives their efforts contribute towards accomplishment. They need guidance and motivation to craft an Action Plan that spells out their collective contributions towards a strategic Objective. Senior leaders will deliver this guidance to work-teams through a multitude of managerial hierarchy so this guidance must be short and clear — not open to 'local thumb-printing' by intermediary managers.

Provide Action Plan guidance that is 80% motivational and inspiring while only 20% instructive and specific. Team members remain the experts at their level of the organization so provide them with the guidance they need to feel included and important in accomplishing the Strategic Plan. Daily business production does not change at the work-team level because a new Strategic Plan has been built and deployed. Their working duties continue. If you are effective in the deployment actions of your Strategic Plan, team members will be able to see how their efforts contribute to strategic endeavors.

Action Plans are informal plans, bullet-style tasks often written on large sheets of paper and displayed in the work-team's area. These Action Plans outline taskings for the team that directly contribute to specific strategic Objectives. Work-team progress towards these taskings, is captured through 'tracking' only, not more complex metrics. Measuring progress of specific Action Plan items will look like the familiar charity-Way fund-raising thermometers, nothing more. The best Action Plans are written over, changes lined through, discussed weekly by work-teams and become energizers for work-team rallying. Action Plans become the team subject over morning coffee, afternoon breaks and create small team excitement.

ESSENTIAL ELEMENTS OF A GOOD ACTION PLAN

- Tasks over and above normal operations
- Accomplished in one year or less
- Specifically assigned to an individual or work-team
- Specifically focused on one strategic Objective
- An estimated completion date
- A simple *tracking* method

CONTENTS OF A SIMPLE WORK-TEAM ACTION PLAN

(Note the responsibility for each element is specified by team member.)

1. Create an improved checklist for receiving materials into the warehouse. (D Skinner) January 1

2. Create an improved warehouse inventory process compatible with the new automation programs mandated. (M Goldstein) March 30

3. Establish 2-person work teams for verifying all external shipments of sensitive materials. (Maurer/ Tegge, Westcott/Meyers) April 1

4. Train all warehouse associates in the new safety and environmental safe-handling procedures. (E Matteo) May 15

5. Implement weekly safety briefings to reduce warehouse accidents and injuries. (G Walter) June 30

6. Increase daily order-fills by 5% on a monthly basis. (J Arendsen) July 15

7. Brief the new Warehouse Supervisor on core process improvement suggestions. (B Armitage) September 1

8. Inventory all warehouse equipment for compliance with OSHA safety requirements. (J Duncan) November 15

X. Deployment — A Deliberate, Holistic Effort to Deploy the Strategic Plan

The deployment of a strategic plan should be a *process*, not just an event. It may include multiple events and may take several weeks to accomplish depending on the size and scope of your organization. Following weeks or months of developing the Strategic Plan, the Chief Executive Officer, President, Director or whomever is your highest level executive, must deploy the Strategic Plan to all stakeholders. This deployment process includes both internal and external stakeholders. The deployment process must be executed by the highest ranking member of the organization. I have seen numerous attempts to deploy Strategic Plans using a trusted 2nd-in-Command, regional Vice Presidents, etc., all with equal fizzle — yes, fizzle, *NOT* sizzle.

A Strategic Plan must cascade through an organization with the patent endorsement of the Chief Executive. The deployment process should become a personal tasking for this senior leader, of course with a multitude of support from all other senior leaders. My point is that this deployment, unlike other operational initiatives must be perceived, received and accepted directly from 'the senior leader.' This direct involvement and the deep respect for the Strategic Plan this process engenders has the same genesis as ensuring the Chief Executive is the central figure in the Strategic Planning Team. Let's face it, if the Boss doesn't have time for this process — who does, who will, are they really serious? Team members are quick to discern disingenuous actions and speeches. Senior leader's credibility is fully transparent during this process, as it should always be.

A complete deployment process will include presentations to all organizational team members — no matter they may be spread across the country in 18 separate locations!

External stakeholders must be invited to special presentations. Inclusion is the watchword in this process. Suppliers, product dealers, distributors, key customers, financial supporters, all should be included — anyone with a stake in the organization's success. This is a step where more-is-better.

There is no better way to convey the importance of team members to the organization and the Strategic Plan than to have the Chief Executive personally hand each associate a copy of the Strategic Plan and then conduct a presentation to explain the details. The deployment process creates a greater opportunity than the mere sharing of your plan. Here is an opportunity to bring team members, middle managers, labor leaders and senior managers together with a focal point on a plan, a process, which can be a win-win for everyone. Here's an opportunity to re-dedicate the Values of the organization, remind distant associates of the core Mission, present a genuine and passionate appeal to craft the unity and alignment required for **good** organizations to become **great** organizations.

For organizations spread across greater territories, your deployment process may be fragmented due to geographic realities. Make these regional presentations real celebrations. Include ceremonies for seniority awards, special employee recognition and organizational achievements. Where better to celebrate new products, increased sales, cost reductions and quality awards? Adding refreshments, product showings and including outside stakeholders like customers, suppliers and financial supporters creates a teaming atmosphere. Including the strategic plan presentation in these celebrations furthers envelops this critical plan into the weave of the corporate culture.

Numerous quality-initiative authors chide us for failing to celebrate often enough as organizations. Old school managers view celebrations as wasteful, time wasters and frivolous. New school leaders celebrate often, showcasing team-based awards, improved processes that reduce production costs or improve efficiencies and champion team members for significant achievements—both within and outside the corporate walls. Make team celebrations the rule, not the exception. Look for reasons to celebrate, team members to champion and awards to present. Who says strategic plan presentations have to be boring and stoic? Team members prosper through the contagion created by dynamic leaders professing new and innovative corporate Goals and Objectives.

XI. Link to Budgets— Success Requires Resource Support

We've all heard the adage, "what the boss checks, gets our attention." This same principle applies to strategic plans and resources. In my research the second most common reason strategic plans failed can be attributed to disconnections between the Strategic Plan and the organization's resource/budget process.

This is just one of the reasons strategic plans fail. Far too many senior executives fall victim to this simple principle. After spending large amounts of efforts and dollars to anchor the best consultants, dazzling facilitators and four-color printed plans—the Strategic Plan fails to be considered in budget projections and monthly budget meetings.

All large military installations and major unit elements spend countless hours wrestling the realities of budget management. The federal government, especially Department of Defense cascade elements, are held to very high budgetary management standards. Forecast allocations must mirror fiscal obligations, each month! Countless checks and balances serve to ensure prudent and reconcilable fiscal actions—an unreported process taxpayers would be very proud to hear about. I was always proud as a taxpayer the way military units managed federal funds—it was not the critical generalizations you read about in the newspaper. I observed detailed, well audited and precise fiscal management. The best military installations and elements, much like the best run private-sector organizations, link their strategic planning process to their budgetary management cycles.

Where I once introduced an inaugural strategic planning process, we modified the monthly budgetary management meeting agenda, to include a complete review of all strategic Objectives being *actioned* during that fiscal year. Each strategic Objective was discussed to ensure no *resourcing* impediments existed or were expected. This was the first action for each month's agenda—ensuring complete resource support for those strategic Objectives the senior leadership had codified as the highest priorities. In this way, senior leaders assured everyone these strategic Objectives were-in-fact the highest priorities and fiscal actions were directed to ensure their success.

As we discussed in an earlier chapter, organizational *behaviors* must reflect the organizational Values. Likewise, organizational *budgetary behaviors* must reflect and support those things, e.g., strategic Objectives, the senior leadership codified as critical. Actions at the highest levels of the organization, especially noticeable by-all budgetary actions, must be true to the Values and stated priorities of any organization. If these Objectives are not resourced, or if they are poorly resourced, what specific message do these lack-of-actions send throughout the organization?

Think about it, organizational Values, codified organizational priorities, demonstrated behaviors, budget actions, leadership integrity—all linked together representing and contributing to organizational alignment. Is this all there is to organizational alignment—oh no, not by a long shot. However, these elements are a huge part of the organizational alignment train.

Build a deliberate bridge between your organization's budget-management process and your Strategic Plan. Including the Chief Fiscal Officer in the senior leadership team formulating your Strategic Plan is a Blinding Flash of the Obvious (BFO). Including this same expert in your Strategic Plan deployment process is also a BFO.

SEVEN

METRICS, THE UGLY WORD, FEAR FOR NO REASON

An often quoted passage is, *"if you can't measure it, you can't manage it."* This is probably very true. Clearly being able to measure processes, trends, actions, achievements and results helps us to actually know what is happening. Too many managers *think* they know what is happening, or not happening, within their areas of responsibility. But do they really know? How do they know? Ever ask someone after they have delivered a profound statement—how do you really know that? Watch their facial expression. After their angst and frustration over your asking such a pointed question, usually there is an embarrassing silence, then another profound statement alluding to their years of experience with such and such...just as you thought, no real answer.

DIFFERENT METRICS FOR DIFFERENT LEVELS OF PLANNING

I think we should clarify a little about metrics before we delve into the specifics and details of creating strategic metrics. The best text I have read on measuring organizational progress is *The Balanced Scorecard* by Kaplan & Norton. While their text is focused on a balanced scorecard approach to organizational measurement, not just strategic measures, Kaplan & Norton present an understandable approach that clarifies many of the mysteries of performance measurement.

PRIMARY LEVELS OF PLANNING RELATE TO LEVELS OF PERSPECTIVE

LONG RANGE
5-20 Years

STRATEGIC
3-5 Years

OPERATIONAL
1-2 Years

TACTICAL
1 year or less

Just as in the various levels of planning, there are various levels of metrics. Strategic plans require *strategic* measures — metrics. Operational plans require operational measures, tactical plans require tactical measures and so on. Metrics at the operational and tactical levels are known as *diagnostic* metrics. You must understand this difference and keep in mind we are going to develop *strategic* measures — not *diagnostic* (operational/tactical level) measures.

A simple example may be:

Working towards my PhD, for me, may be a strategic objective. Monitoring my heart-rate, blood pressure and respiration rate is also important — because if any of these measures drops to zero, my strategic pursuits become history, I have passed on! So I must have a *strategic* measure that monitors my *strategic* Objective (PhD), possibly including Phases of required schooling, surveys, dissertations, etc., to effectively manage my progress. The measures and metrics associated with my heart-rate, blood pressure and respiration rate are *operational* (diagnostic) level metrics — for *operational* level activities. Clearly both of these kinds of measures are important — but we are only focused on **strategic measures**, metrics for **strategic planning** and for specifically measuring strategic Objectives.

All organizations use and require diagnostic metrics for operational and tactical level activities and production. It is these measures that allow us to conduct and manage daily business! I am not advocating anyone stop using diagnostic metrics — they are critical. However, diagnostic metrics are not in the strategic context in which we are developing and deploying a strategic plan. Our discussion of metrics within this strategic context is focused on developing metrics that measure, progress towards or regress away from, our strategic Objectives. Keep your thoughts in the strategic realm. Remember these different levels of planning and metrics, strategic metrics vs. diagnostic metrics, a huge difference.

You should conduct enough independent research of metrics to understand the different perspectives of metrics. *Leading* metrics, those metrics that can be used to forecast future performance based on known data points, can be very useful in strategic planning. Lagging metrics, those metrics capturing historical data can also be useful for documenting, establishing baselines and comparison analyses.

After painstakingly developing the strategic Objectives you must develop an associated metric to measure your progress. Remember, we don't measure strategic Goals, only strategic Objectives. We used the SMART criteria for creating our Objectives, M representing the *Measurable* element. Writing strategic Objectives in a way that makes them measurable will serve you well a hundred times over.

The eleven developmental steps presented in chapter 6 must be followed sequentially. After crafting all of the strategic Goals, then all of the supporting strategic Objectives and their respective Strategies, you should build a metric for each strategic Objective. In reviewing your strategic Objectives, the first order of business is to determine exactly *what it is* you are going to measure. At times, gleaning out the elements for measure is not always obvious. Again, group dynamics provide the best forum for this sorting process. As one person's thoughts provoke another's vision, soon the key elements for measure are clear. Look at this example:

"Develop and adopt an updated Gun Safety public information campaign throughout the Capitol Region by September 30, 2013."

- Elements of measure here will be the developmental/adoption steps of the Gun Safety public information campaign.
- The 'target date' of Sept 30, 2013 will also be shown on the metric.

We could simply create a go/no go measure — did the public information campaign get developed? Yes or No? A simplistic measure like this is only 'tracking,' far less than creating a complete metric. If we used a simple tracking measure we would only be able to measure completion, not actual progress. Metrics for purposes of strategic planning have three or more 'measures.' Time is often one measure. Developmental steps, elements, Phases or measured quantities may be another 'measure.' Groups, Regions, sales volume numbers, quantities of orders, etc. may be another

---

METRICS REMINDERS TO ENHANCE CLARITY AND MEANING

There are numerous rules for creating *useful* strategic metrics, these are some of my guidelines:

- Once you determine the 'elements of measure,' try several different chart types to see which type illuminates your status the best.

- Use automation 'macros' applications to make creating the metric easier

- Singular strategic Objective focus only, data + time element + history

- 10 second clarity rule

- 'Good' arrows (↑↓)indicating desired direction for progress

- 'As of date' adds relevance and currency

- Indicate a Point of Contact for data questions, or clarity, or person responsible for posting data

- Indicate metric posting frequency

- Include a comments box for reminders and interpretation ease; "seasonal trends suggest higher returns during next Quarter"; "Fiscal close-out completes Sept 30th" 'measure.' Including a historical comparative, i.e., a quantity, previous Phases dates, sales or production figures, or performance data as a backdrop or comparative measure, can make the metric more valuable.

Clients always ask *"what's the best type of chart to use?"* There is no universal answer for this. Every set of data is best portrayed by a different style of chart. Numerous texts explain and clarify the best use for various chart styles. The list is endless and expanded by every new automation program or macro. Pie or coin charts are great for illuminating parts or portions of something, 100% equaling the entire pie or coin. Stacked bar graphs and column graphs are great for portraying 2-3 dimensions of data at the same time, as in Phase completions. Pyramid charts may portray easy comparisons of similar groups or efforts, various sizes depicting easy differences in totals. Line charts illustrate a protracted process, clearly indicating plateaus of time or data lags. Venn diagrams best portray overlaps in impacts, groups, actions, etc.

There is enough information and different schools of thought on data chart-types to become an expert on metrics—of which I am not. Metrics for me are merely a window to measure strategic progress or regress, nothing more. I strongly urge those engaged in metrics development to casually research a few texts to become more familiar with the nuances of each chart type. Most organizations have team members that excel with charting automation programs. I encourage senior leadership teams to tap this readily-available staff expertise for the purpose of assisting in metric chart-typing. Insist everyone on the senior leadership team developing the strategic plan, be a part of the metric discussions, decisions, selecting the 'elements of measure' etc. Inclusion is the watchword here. Don't delegate this important element to someone outside the strategic planning development team. You must keep the co-authorship torch burning to the very end of the development process.

Be careful not to go overboard on metrics. Some metrics developers portray data too detailed and too confusing to be useful. Bear in mind the difference between useful and meaningful. Sure, we can build metrics with excruciating detail that are meaningful—but only after a full 5 minute review! Don't be tempted by more-is-better thinking, for strategic metrics, less-is-better mostly. Keep strategic metrics useful.

I tell my clients, if an external stakeholder cannot read and understand your metric within 10 seconds it is too complicated or poorly designed. I'm not talking about an expert in your specific specialty, I'm talking about one of your customers, suppliers or bankers. The *USA Today* newspaper uses very good metrics. Review a few of the metrics found in the daily newspaper, notice how much information you can retrieve from them in just 10 seconds. Often these are shown in just black and white. People tend to want to apply color to metrics. It's OK, but reproduces poorly for copies and of course color-blind readers can't differentiate various values. Black and white reproduction with shading works equally well.

METRICS, NOT JUST TRACKING

It is best to understand the difference in metrics and simple tracking. There is a significant difference between these two types of performance measuring and a different purpose for using metrics and *tracking*. When monitoring Action Plans, those one-year or less, informal plans accomplished at the work-team level of the organization, use a measuring process known as *tracking*. Tracking is monitoring just one measure. A good example of *tracking* is the large 'thermometer style' signs found at street intersections indicating the percentage of funding pledged for certain charity-Way campaigns. These are very effective, quick to understand and require no interpretation. Tracking has a valid use and should be used for Action Plans. This is *tracking* only, these are not metrics.

For managing strategic Objectives we use strategic metrics, a compound group of measures, usually including a target date, a time-measure element, comparative data and data labels that clearly portray the present status of progress towards a strategic Objective. Metrics usually include three or four different measures and sometimes as many as eight elements of measure.

EIGHT

MOMENTUM – KEEPING IT MOVING

ACTION PLANS—HOW, WHY, WHEN AND BY WHOM

Every great organization is comprised of associates, team members, employees, direct-reports—the people that create, build, recommend, suggest, produce and craft the very products and services the Mission statement describes. Many are organized into work-teams, groups, sections, divisions, departments and shift-groups. I'm talking about the smallest groupings of team members that operate as a 'unit,' performing a similar service or adding a specific 'value' to the organizational product or service. This is where a strategic plan grows roots and takes grip on the organization.

How do the strategic intentions and desires of senior leaders actually become part of the daily operations and activities? Where do we transcend the operational realm and **grow the strategic actions** required to move towards our Vision? The answer is at the work-team level, those groupings of team members organized by function, service or specialty.

The actions that keep the products moving and the sales activities that create the forward movement of our vast products and services do not and cannot quit moving. The hum of daily workplace *business*, whatever your product or service is, continues on as it does every day. So then, how and where do we inject those things that empower and energize our strategic direction? Action Plans. Action Plans are informal short duration plans *added* to the operational taskings and routine actions of work-teams. These plans are *in addition to*, not in lieu of, normal activities. Action Plans are created by work-teams, ideally as a collective effort, which are executed simultaneously with regular job performance. Think in terms of *integrated and concurrent efforts* for regular work activities.

BASIC ACTION PLAN SUCCESS BUILDERS

I like to see work-teams create Action Plans on large 'butcher block' style sheets of paper. Simple and bold felt-marker bullet-style actions listed in sequential order. Action Plans posted in the immediate work areas and walls seem to be the most successful. These visual reminders can motivate and energize small team momentum. Keep these rules in mind when crafting Action Plans:

RULES FOR ACTION PLANS

- Must be accomplished within 1 year or less
- Tasks *over and above* normal operations
- Specifically assigned to an individual or team
- Specifically focused on one strategic Objective
- Must have a completion date for each task
- Should include a method for tracking progress

How many Action Plans does one work-team create? A separate Action Plan should be created for every strategic Objective that particular work-team directly supports. Conceivably a work-team might have a half dozen Action Plans being accomplished at any one time. As a work-team reviews the Strategic Plan to determine which strategic Objectives apply directly to them, other strategic Objectives that are not directly linked to their efforts, can be set aside.

I have also seen Action Plans created at higher levels of the organization, which apply to the entire workforce. Action Plans at these macro levels rarely conger the same synergy and enthusiasm. There is something special about an informal plan, crafted by a handful of associates, which bonds and energizes the pride of 'our group.' There is nothing wrong with building Action Plans at higher levels, but it is more difficult to create these using a collective effort. Action Plans developed for the entire workforce often convey a top-down feeling, just another mandate. One of the greatest values of small-team created Action Plans is the feeling of ownership and participation in the overall Strategic Plan.

LOCATIONS OF TEAM MEMBERS REQUIRES SPECIAL TECHNIQUES

Organizations with team members spread across vast geographic areas have special challenges to team unity and ownership of the Strategic Plan. When groups of associates are concentrated at factories, plants, installations or hubs, the decentralized array is more easily overcome. Where associates are home-based or spread among numerous small offices, the quest to create co-ownership and team synergy for the Strategic Plan is much more challenging.

In these situations the involvement of the Chief Executive cannot be overstated. Just as I discussed in the *deployment process* for a Strategic Plan, the excitement and enthusiasm created by senior leaders can overcome geographic fragmentation of the workforce. Creative and additional means, of developing and maintaining focus and alignment with the strategic direction, must be used. Posters and reminders for associates can be great visual prompts to keep everyone's attention on distant Goals and Objectives. Remember, while informal Action Plans at the work-team level are plans of one year or less in duration, strategic Objectives are usually 1-3 years in duration. A deliberate and well thought-out approach must be taken in maintaining everyone's attention and interest on these longer-term targets.

That age-old methodology for keeping managers abreast of staff and activity dynamics, known as *'management by walking around,'* can pay extra dividends in your efforts to align strategic momentum. Asking impromptu questions and initiating casual conversations with team members and supervisors creates an ambient atmosphere of *what's important.* People remember those things the boss mentions, asks about and surprises them with. The informal communications brought about by a few questions carry the message faster than the corporate newsletter or electronic bulletin board.

Pride is another special element at play in this process that can be utilized. Work-teams will demonstrate and exhibit professional pride in every opportunity *you create* for them. Asking work-teams to post their Action Plan progress on the walls of their work areas generates huge displays of *our team is best.* When you can stimulate the pride factor every employee has, you can move mountains. Many will doubt my suggestion and pass off the belief that everyone harbors this innate virtue. Make no mistake about it, where and how you awaken the pride factor in almost every team member, can exponentially leverage their talents, motivations and energy. Time and time again I have observed people overachieve even their own optimistic estimates — for almost everything and anything, with almost nothing. Production improvements, process improvements, cost reductions and product improvements can be taken to unexpected levels where pride is abundant. The onus remains on leaders to develop opportunities and be the catalyst for team pride. This *leading* action is a key delineation between managers and leaders.

Simple geography does not have to be an impediment to organizational synergy or alignment. It does however add another dimension to the approach and efforts made to establish and maintain these critical elements. If staff visits to distant plants or the far corners of the factory are focused on people, not production numbers and manufacturing glitches, what will be the new results? I contend where we focus on people, their needs, their aspirations and suggestions, these other empirical management points of focus will require far less attention.

IMPROVEMENTS IMPLY CHANGE

How does your organization manage change? Evolving and growing organizations must manage change well. Organizations that do not manage change well are often stagnating and dying. A casual read through any major newspaper will remind us quickly which organizations are doing each. Management and motivation gurus have told us for years, *"either an organization is changing or it is dying."* Corporate news of the past 5 years underscores the levity of just such an assessment.

Introducing an inaugural Strategic Plan, or deploying a new Compendium to your current Strategic Plan, signifies change to every member of the team. While presenting an ambient concern for many team members, here lies a huge

ty for leadership, specifically senior leaders astute
...ances of human behavior. What a great opportunity to grab the *attention and energies* of team members and
align the greatness of possibility? I spent my 36-plus career
years in a *training organization*, not a learning organization.
The opportunities for aligning teams with organizational
Values and personal ambitions were vast - and mostly lost.
Leaders focused on *things* instead of opportunities, growth
and possibility. How hugely different it could have been.
Sullivan and Harper in their great text on leadership in organizations, *Hope Is Not A Method*, outline several leadership skills required for future organizational success:

- *Leaders who can scan and focus — who can maintain
  a broad personal outlook but can relate what they are
  seeing and learning in a purposeful way.*

- *Leaders who can create strategic architecture based on
  the cornerstones of values and vision.*

- *Leaders who can see patterns where others cannot and
  have the courage to decide and act quickly.*

- *Leaders who can lead in a learning organization,
  networking, influencing and inspiring.*

- *Leaders who are personally empowered by technology.*

- *Leaders who can teach and develop subordinates.*

- *Leaders who can make the human dimension central to
  their organization.*

Anyone who hasn't read Sullivan and Harper's text
should do so. It is iconic in understanding the pitfalls and
challenges of organizations dealing with change, transition
and the leadership catalyst required to transcend both.

CLIMATE, CULTURE AND **WIFM**

A Strategic Plan can be the pivotal opportunity to escalate a simple *climate* change to a sweeping organizational *cultural* change. When lecturing I often use the example of turning off the lights in the room as a climate change. Climate changes are quick, usually easy to affect and often temporary in duration. Cultural changes on the other hand are all the opposite. Cultural changes within an organization can take 3-5 years to become institutionalized. Cultural changes require great efforts, continuous reinforcement and must be demonstrated through both personal and organizational behaviors. Cultural changes often create new environments that are long lasting and in the best circumstances become indelible to the fabric of the organization. Likewise, in the worst cases, culture can also become indelible to the fabric of the organization.

Changes, especially a new focus or the sweeping improvements brought about by a Strategic Plan have large impacts on people. People at every level of the organization are impacted, even those postulating the change. Is every organization ready for such dramatic change? Is every team member ready for these kinds of changes? Remember, people don't naturally gravitate to change. Change creates stress, discomfort and a fog of ambiguity. People ponder the impact of such change on them, their families and their personal agendas. *What's in it for me* (WIFM) is an element alive and well in the minds of many coworkers. You must anticipate and be prepared to deal with these certainties. Even as you announce a new strategic plan, team members begin to imagine the consequences—mostly with negative assumptions.

GREAT EXPECTATIONS

Another impact on the people in your workforce, created by *the change* of a Strategic Plan or a Revision to a Strategic Plan, is **an escalation in personal expectations**. We are all victims of this almost subconscious ratcheting-up of our acceptable thresholds. While change creates a certain new stress on us, we also elevate our sense of *what is fair, due and proper* given this new condition. Ever get in line to receive a free coupon for a hugely popular new product, just to have the coupons exhausted just as you progressed to the head of the line? How did it make you feel? Disappointed? Were you let down? Were you mad as hell? Why? You weren't really owed a *coupon.* The coupon was not really an entitlement—it was merely a new condition you felt expectant to receive. You weren't actually cheated out of anything—although you may have felt cheated. This is the same feeling many people feel when we attempt to improve their work environment—and the improvement fails to materialize. Its akin to your favorite restaurant selling their last filet mignon to a friend you came to the restaurant with—now you must make another entrée selection. This creates a new disappointment? While this rise in personal expectations can create disappointment if not realized, it can also fuel the fire of excitement and elations, where leaders deliver satisfaction at this newly heightened level.

Anticipate the questions and assumptions team members will make. One of my clients, where I was facilitating an inaugural Strategic Plan, expected a stormy reception by rank-and-file associates. Asked how *we* might handle the certain onslaught of pessimism and difficult questions, as we traveled to numerous regional deployment presentations and Q&A discussions, I suggested the Chief Executive simply present the Strategic Plan as an 85% effort. I suggested he explain this plan reflects the best strategic plan possible as an initial effort. Then I suggested, he should ask every audience to contribute their best thoughts and suggestions directly back to him, the Chief Executive, through every means available. As I recall, we encountered very few difficult questions and none of the 'push-back' anticipated. As team members learned their suggestions and ideas were *welcomed by the boss*, the much-anticipated anxiety failed to materialize.

An initial strategic plan may be at best an 85-90% product. After all, the initial Environmental Scan, the Staff Es timates, the Planning Assumptions and the Alternate and Probable Futures, developed at the onset of the strategic plan development are scientific estimates, only truisms, not finite certainties. Revised or updated strategic plans can improve to be 90-95% planning products and that is about as good as can be achieved in strategic planning. The constantly changing business conditions, that dynamic strategic environment all organizations must operate within, precludes eventual perfection. Having said that, if only all organizations were operating on plans that proved to be 95% accurate, think how much improved business and economic climates would be.

MAINTAINING FORWARD PROGRESS

An excellent way to keep work teams focused and every team moving forward is to ask work-teams to present brief overviews of their Action Plans to their supervisor one-level up. Short presentations with little or no notice preclude a lot of time invested in presentation preparation and fuss. First line leaders should be capable of explaining Action Plan progress by their teams and the tracking systems they are using to monitor progress on an impromptu basis. Whenever possible allow all of the team members to be present as their leader overviews the work-team progress with his or her supervisor. This is another great opportunity for crediting and showing appreciation for team members. Team member pride will cast away any angst created by this small tasking. Ask pertinent questions and watch how fast small teams achieve their portions of strategic Objectives. These short reviews will provide valuable information for staff updates and conversational (situational) awareness. Remember, these brief reviews are focused on just the *Action Plan* progress, not the overall strategic Objective progress, itself a much greater endeavor. This is another reason to use large plain paper for outlining Action Plans — portability, clarity and ease of line-through updates.

SURVEYS, SENSING SESSIONS AND JOB SATISFACTION

Another excellent way to maintain organizational momentum is to survey all of your team members to determine, document and monitor their job satisfaction. I have used the free downloadable survey, *Are We making Progress?*, developed by the US Department of Commerce, National Institute of Standards and Testing (NIST), numerous times with excellent results (http://www.baldrige.nist.gov). It is a simple, quick to complete survey that can establish an excellent baseline of employee job satisfaction. It is written to discern employee job satisfaction and asks numerous questions about the employee's knowledge of organizational direction. Once all associates have taken this survey, you have an excellent baseline for annual surveys using this same survey instrument. I've used this same survey on an annual basis to monitor improvements in job satisfaction. This is a very simple method and still very effective.

Will all of the team members be excited and happy where strategic planning and strategic direction are codified in their workplace? One particular client, a dear friend of mine, the Vice President for Operations of a giant food service provider in healthcare facilities, long-term care facilities and retirement homes, was sharing with me the trials and tribulations of trying to keep all of their customers satisfied. Extolling the challenges of customer satisfaction she shared, " . . . *some residents want the Brunswick Stew thicker, others want it thinner, for some it is too cool, for others it is too hot . . . .,*" a never ending saga of trying to please thousands of elderly residents and patients—and of course the Brunswick Stew is never quite the same as how *they* used to make it! So, no, not every team member will find complete happiness and excitement in your workplace—and that's OK.

Sensing sessions are a unique opportunity for senior leaders to listen directly to organizational members, away from supervisory influence. A visiting CEO, CFO or Vice President will prosper greatly by sitting down with 8-20 associates in a private setting. Absent other supervisors, simply question and listen to team members. Ask those questions only team members know. Are the organizational Vision, Mission and Values percolating throughout the ranks of the organization? Do these associates understand what the latest critical issue for success is this year? What is the actual organizational culture? Are the organizational Values demonstrated by managers, by co-workers? Keep their answers separate from names and locations and departments. Be firm is informing intermediary supervisors this was a private session, not subject to questions and prodding. When a CEO conducts 10 or more of these sensing sessions throughout the organization, a clear picture of real issues will emerge. Whether real or imagined, perceptions remain the team member's reality and reflect organizational culture.

CRITERIA FOR PERFORMANCE EXCELLENCE

The website referenced previously, (http://www.baldrige.nist.gov), also contains the Criteria for Performance Excellence, you should use the Baldrige National Quality Program link. This is the quality criteria for assessing performance excellence within organizations. Using such comprehensive criteria and then competing in the Malcolm Baldrige Quality Award Program, either at the State or National level, will improve any organization immeasurably. The Self-Assessment tool will be very revealing, if not damning, initially. I encourage all of my clients to use this free tool to improve their organization. I was skeptical myself many, many years ago, then having experienced it first hand, as part of an organization that had no previous experience with Malcolm Baldrige Quality Award criteria, was more than impressive. It became a pivotal point for that organization and was central to ratcheting the organization up to levels of excellence unheard of in Public Sector organizations.

I tell clients this tirelessly, read and study—really study the text by Sullivan and Harper, *Hope Is Not A Method* and then employ the Malcolm Baldrige Award Criteria, *Criteria for Performance Excellence*. If your organizational performance doesn't double I'll be very surprised. If you use an external facilitator, trained in these protocols, to assist your organization, you will see exponential organizational performance improvements. If you combine these two investments, that's really what these tools are, organizational investments you know, with a comprehensive strategic planning process—your organizational performance will exceed your greatest expectations! Believe me, this is really true. I am so convinced this is true, I use it as the basis for my consulting fees. I actually bet my consulting fees on this very premise—with every client!

NINE

OFF-SITES AND THE REVIEW PROCESS

THE REVIEW CYCLE

An important element in every Strategic Plan should be a committed review cycle and process. Clearly outline for all stakeholders the cycle for the Strategic Plan review and revisions. Describe the interval for updating, the precise process that will be used and exactly who will be included in the review activity. Make no secrets about your review intentions and I absolutely recommend a transparent strategic planning process throughout. Share with all stakeholders your entire strategic planning process, including the cyclic review process. I want to emphasize a committed review process — as in all elements of a strategic plan — demonstrated actions to support everything you codify in the Strategic Plan are important.

How Often, A Cyclic Process?

The dynamics of the strategic environment dictate strategic plans be revised and updated on a cyclic basis. *How* you do this is as important as *when* you do this and *with whom*. Understanding why updating a strategic plan is necessary is paramount to the strategic planning process. The constantly changing, evolving strategic environment alters the best intentions and direction of every organization. Technologies that create the best advantages and efficiencies today are lost on the emerging technologies and their impacts tomorrow. As most of us would acknowledge, organizations are either changing or dying. Developing and maintaining plans to provide continual guidance under these conditions is difficult and complex at best. Failing to keep planning actions abreast of changing strategic environments is failure by in-action.

Understanding the premise strategic plans must be kept reasonably current, how often should strategic plans actually be revised. No hard and fast rule here, but revisions must be made at responsible intervals or as soon as possible after significant changes in the organization's strategic environment. I advise my clients a 12–18 month interval is best, unless significant shifts in the strategic environment dictate an earlier timeframe. I have purposely qualified the vernacular; we are talking about the **Organization's** strategic environment. Every organization operates within the context of a unique strategic environment, defined by itself and its stakeholders, consciously or not.

Updated by Whom?

In chapter 3 I presented the various ways to create your strategic plan development team. These same concepts apply to the senior leadership team selected to update the Strategic Plan. Yes, there will be some changes in personnel. Retirements, transfers and scheduling realities create some loss of continuity between the development team and the review team assembling 12-18 months later. That's OK. New team members that have prepared and are well versed in the Strategic Plan and experienced with the organization or domain will join the process seamlessly. I should caution that whatever composition style (i.e., senior leadership, cross section, Regional representation, etc.) was used for the development team, using a similar composition is probably best for the review process.

I strongly recommended a professional facilitator be used to orchestrate and guide your team through the building stages of strategic planning. All of the same reasons apply to your updating process. Use an external facilitator, one trained in strategic planning. This is not the time to use Mr. Doright from the marketing department because he has some facilitator experience. Knowing the speed-bumps and potential potholes of team-based strategic planning will expedite and ease your strategic planning updating process. Free the members of your senior leadership team from their normal roles and subdue the pecking-order as much as possible. While professional respect for seniors will always be present, try to reduce the distance between people such respect creates, as much as possible.

Allow an outside facilitator to keep the team disciplined to the group-rules agreed upon at the onset. Don't task the Vice President or another senior staffer to accomplish all of the side-bar logistic details of meals, recreation activities eting room set-up. Use a facilitator to work through ncillary taskings, in addition to the core meetings and discussions. Let your facilitator select a seasoned recorder trained to capture ideas and verbal offerings as several leaders share their thoughts simultaneously. A good facilitator will ensure the recorder is not drawn into the group's discussions. Spending a few dollars for outside professionals to free-up your regular go-to people for these administrative duties is money well spent.

OFF-SITES

If an ounce of prevention is worth is worth a pound of cure — it follows a relaxed and creative atmosphere for crafting an organizational future is worth a reasonable expense. Select a location away from your normal business environs. Create an atmosphere of trust, isolation and focus for attendees. This doesn't have to be an extravagant pilgrimage, though an environment that relaxes and frees the attendees from routine thoughts provides greater results. Keep in mind, normal everyday work routines keep most people within an operational realm. In order for people to extract themselves from instinctual thinking processes and routine focus, you must bring them to the strategic realm using several tools.

Physical atmosphere and scheduling are a few ways to re-direct their routine mental tendencies. Additional ways include using a relaxed dress code and hosting group activities. Announce in advance notifications and agendas, business-casual will be the expected dress. Where not everyone shares a common golfing or exercise passion, arrange for guided walks around the facility grounds or shopping trips to local markets. Gathering around a popular football game TV viewing or visiting a local attraction generates valuable discussions, verbal side-bars and sharing. Often these side benefits occur between team members that normally work closely together — further broadening the team fabric. Teaming has many faces and organized socializing will bind a team and build trust with little effort. Except for a handful of senior leaders, the strategic realm is atypical for many of your review team members. Talk about these differences in perspective as a lead-in to group discussions.

AGENDAS AND ADVANCE MATERIALS

Create and share the Off-Site Agenda several weeks ahead of your off-site workshop. Include administrative details and group expectations. People usually don't like surprises and late notifications and agenda surprises don't build any trust or clear minds. The last thing anyone wants to create are *hostile* attendees irritated by a lack of time to get properly prepared or surprised by special events and a lack of proper attire. Be clear about what costs are reimbursable and which costs are not. Eliminate surprises everyway you can and accommodate your team members in the same way you expect to be accommodated when taking a weekend getaway.

When providing advance materials for a strategic planning or updating workshop, make the time and effort to provide presentation slides in both hard-copy and electronic format. Paper handouts offer the chance to make impromptu notes without computers. Electronic formats are great for advance distribution while paper copies provided at the workshop provide note-taking convenience. In addition, consider placing just three slides on each page and make the copies back-to-back, allowing enough space for note-taking and highlighting. Every time I see slides grouped on handouts as 6-per page, I am reminded how people tend to gravitate to efficiency before effectiveness. Low hanging fruit always seems to be picked *near-sightedly* first.

DISTRACTIONS, ELIMINATE THE COMPETITION

Yes, I know many people prefer to make their notations on computers, but a roomful of flipped-up computers can really slow down and kill group interaction. Do you really want to underwrite a 3-day leadership retreat, hire a facilitator than watch your group discussions fizzle because everyone is focused on their laptop computer? Strategic planning is a team sport and the synergy and thought provocation created through facilitated and interactive group-think is valuable in multiple ways.

To ensure group focus and eliminate distracters ask participants to place all electronic devices outside the door in a basket. Cellular telephones, pagers and the like have a key place in our daily lives, but quickly become distractions for everyone. Even the most senior leaders will balk at the suggestion, but a good facilitator has learned these lessons before — save yourself and others the frustration. Time after time a team member returning late from a break asks the very same question just discussed by the large group — 10 more minutes lost to inconsideration. Promptness in starting and adhering to break periods assures everyone a chance to make critical telephone calls when necessary. An excellent way to keep your group focused is to discuss these distractions as part of the workshop rules established at the beginning of the workshop. Post these rules on the wall and refer to them throughout your discussions. Being able to guide the group through these awkward discussions is another job of your facilitator.

The professionalism and discipline demonstrated during an off-site workshop sends a message. This is quality team time. A relaxed pace, great surroundings and informal atmosphere doesn't have to be unprofessional and become a gaggle. Team members have to know while this process is a serious effort, it can still be fun without digressing to displaced chaos.

A Thorough Review Process

Conducting periodic off-site reviews of a strategic plan is required to maintain strategic currency and the appropriate strategic focus for any organization. During off-site reviews your strategic planning team should collectively review every facet of the current Strategic Plan and the strategic planning process.

Items to Periodically Review Off-Site

- Recently updated Environmental Scan staff estimates.

- Discuss the initial SWOT analysis listings and any added or deleted elements no longer valid.

- Verify the initial SWOT element listings by priority.

- Review previous Alternative Futures to validate their accuracy.

- Discuss the previous strategic Goals and revise where necessary.

- Discuss the previous strategic Objectives and revise them where necessary.

- Add any emerging strategic Goals and Objectives, ensuring use of the SMART criteria for Objectives.

- Revise or delete any Strategies no longer valid.

ITEMS TO PERIODICALLY REVIEW OFF-SITE
(CONTINUED)

- Review every metric for each strategic Objective and adjust elements of measure, scales or chart-type as needed.

- Update the Target Matrix or Success Matrix in accordance with new or revised completion dates for strategic Objectives.

- Discuss the budgetary and resourcing meetings inclusion of strategic Objectives, how they are working and any adjustments required.

- Review the previous deployment process, employee reception and reactions.

- Review survey results from organizational team members.

- Discuss the previous Strategic Plan publication effectiveness.

- Build consensus for the type of updated Strategic Plan, Compendium or Update publication as a product of your review.

Almost all of these preparatory steps can be accomplished by the Strategic Planning Team prior to an actual Off-Site Review. Having the recorder document key questions, highlight unresolved issues and create handouts for the Off-Site of unresolved issues will greatly streamline your group efforts during the actual Off-Site review process.

Most organizations would prosper by following country singer Dolly Parton's simple practice, "If I see something dragging, sagging or bagging, I get it fixed."

TEN

REVISIONS AND COMPENDIUMS

CONSTANT CHANGE, THE PLANNER'S NEMESIS

Almost everything in the organization's strategic environment is changing — both inside and outside the organization. New technologies obsolete equipment purchases of just five years ago. Automation speed and emerging programs modify processes and procedures continually. Market shifts in consumer demand and the globalization of product markets keep business, industry and education communities in a constant state of flex. Strategic plans must be flexible and provide organizational guidance — reflective of the dynamic world around them.

We established earlier in this text strategic plans represent a three to five year planning scope. This is the planning scope for establishing and setting strategic direction for the organization. Long-range plans have a planning scope of five to twenty years while operational plans generally provide guidance for one to two years.

Although the planning scope for strategic plans is three to five years we cannot expect a strategic plan to remain viable for that entire period. Therefore, I recommend strategic plans be reviewed and updated every 12-18 months. Upon the completion of a thorough review, updated and revised strategic guidance should be provided to all stakeholders. While the initial strategic direction remains mostly constant, some variation can be expected as a result of the ever-changing strategic environment. While it is true you should keep a strategic plan current through a cyclic review process, you also shouldn't create large-scale confusion or the perception the strategic direction is radically changing. Associates are always searching for evidence strategic plans are a *flavor-of-the-month event*, not a continuing process. You must maintain strategic plan currency, without harpooning the strategic direction.

Change for the sake of change is without value. If after a complete review, your leadership team finds no significant updates are required, by all means continue using the same Strategic Plan until the next review — or until a significant change in the strategic environment. My experience has shown strategic plans require a formal review and a 10%-20% revision every 12-18 months. Most strategic Goals remain the same with a few new supporting strategic Objectives added. Many strategic Objectives remain the same with a few modifications of the supporting Strategies. Obviously the Action Plans, which break down and document the doable steps for work-teams, change each year as they retain a planning scope of one year or less.

AFTER THE REVIEW, WHAT'S NEXT?

After you complete a comprehensive off-site review, there are several potential products and actions to be accomplished. Some organizations publish a completely new Strategic Plan, changing the title to reflect the current edition. Others prefer to publish a new Annex containing the *revised elements* for use with the original Strategic Plan. I believe the best way to convey this revised strategic *direction*, this updated strategic guidance, is to publish a revised Strategic Plan in the form of a Compendium. I recommend a Compendium because it is easy to retain a visual nexus to the original Strategic Plan thereby reducing the confusion for most stakeholders. This could be very similar in design and layout to the original Strategic Plan to convey planning continuity to readers and stakeholders alike. Consider modifying the title slightly to project the new Compendium as a sister-publication, linked but clearly updated. Using similar graphics designs, colors and titles creates a bridge for readers. Titles like, *Compendium 2010 to Corporate Vision 2012*, transition the reader easily. *Annual Update to Future Path 2011* or *Revision III to the University of Excellence Strategic Plan* may also be effective.

Using explanatory paragraphs in your revised Strategic Plan convey the review process that was used and the carry-over theme you want to maintain. Be clear about the necessity for updating the Strategic Plan and reassure stakeholders of the successes achieved thus far. Clarify the most significant changes to the organization's strategic environment and how these changes impact the organization. Transparency in strategic plans often returns ambient benefits. If I haven't emphasized it enough already in this text, I will say it again. The Chief Executive must be the largest cheerleader for the organization's Strategic Plan and must constantly market it to all stakeholders, internal and external.

After publishing a revision to the Strategic Plan, I strongly recommend duplicating the *deployment process* executed for the initial Strategic Plan. If the previous deployment process included the Chief Executive with other senior leaders traveling to geographically regionalized locations for presenting a brief overview, then duplicate this deployment process again. This repeating process includes the benefit of being able to portray the strategic Objective metrics (from the inaugural Strategic Plan) and the real organizational results associates worked so hard to achieve. Team members love to hear directly from the CEO and ask questions about strategic realities. When the Chief Executive personally hands each team member their own copy of the Strategic Plan and thanks them for their efforts and ideas, most recipients become prideful participants. Engendering team member's pride and loyalty are priceless in an age where labor relationships and the quality of products and services can spell the difference between organizational success and failure.

As I suggested previously in this text, these kind of meetings with team members are great opportunities (spell huge) for crediting, presenting seniority awards, team-based quality awards and building community relationships. You should invite local members of the media, local government representatives and other external stakeholders to these events. Provide Press Releases and develop a celebratory atmosphere. The benefits received will exceed your highest expectations.

SPREAD THE WORD

One of my clients producing a Strategic Plan for the very first time accepted my recommendation to electronically post all of the Strategic Plan's metrics (one for each of the strategic Objectives) on every team member's computers. This single icon, designed to replicate the Strategic

Plan, allowed every associate the opportunity to monitor the organizational progress. Everyone, regardless of their station, shared the very same visibility as the CEO, of strategic Objective's status. This same portal included *a hot button icon* to submit suggestions by any team member desiring to do so. These suggestions were collected and included in the next monthly budget meeting or annual update off-site as appropriate. Like the assembly line rope-pull at Saturn, this electronic porthole, with a suggestion box icon, gave everyone an equal opportunity to participate, suggest, observe and embrace pride in *their* organization's progress. Sometimes just providing the opportunity to opine and being encouraged to do so, is enough inclusiveness to dissipate angst and pushback. This creates a continual improvement process where everyone is empowered to contribute. Inclusion of team members engenders a genuine feeling of *teaming* and underscores a senior leader's commitment to the organization.

This same client chose to publish an annual Compendium for their Strategic Plan, *Vision 2005*. After publishing their inaugural Strategic Plan, then three additional annual Compendiums named for the succeeding years, they published their next Strategic Plan, *Vision 2010*.

MARKETING, CHEERLEADING AND TEAMS

All of these follow-on activities I have described: the cyclic review process; the publication of an updated or revised Strategic Plan; a recurring deployment process; face-to-face presentations by the Chief Executive with team members; opportunities to suggest improvements; portholes to the strategic progress through sharing metrics; verbal acknowledgements and crediting; all contribute to the gradual improvement of the organization's *culture*. While improving the culture of the organization can take three to five years, it almost nothing—and can reap exponential dividends. People easily identify genuine efforts made to improve *their* organization. Demonstrated behaviors of real leadership will create proactive actions and hallmark outstanding leaders.

LEADERSHIP PERSPECTIVES CORELATE TO DIFFERENT LEVELS OF PLANNING

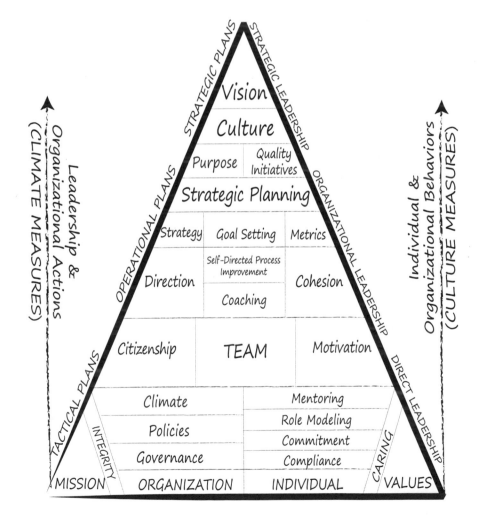

ELEVEN

WHY STRATEGIC PLANS FAIL

WHERE *IS* THE STRATEGIC PLAN?

I should qualify this chapter title and remind you, many organizations simply do not have a Strategic Plan. There are many reasons for this and most of them embarrassingly poor. A few of the many I've heard before:

"We were growing so fast we never stopped to think about what our future looked like or might be."

"Our organization was doing so well, we didn't expect the market to die off so fast, it left us flat-footed and with no alternative products or markets to carry us forward."

"We believed our Business Plan was all we would need for the next several years, now looking back on it, I guess we really didn't have any plans beyond that and that was 7 years ago."

"None of us really knew much about strategic plans and we didn't hire anyone else to help us with one. Now we wished we would have, we were growing so much, lately we've just stagnated and seem to be stuck in a sales and marketing rut."

The percentage of small businesses that have strategic plans remains small. The number of medium sized and larger organizations having a strategic plan is greater but still not significantly so. The Education Sector; universities; colleges and larger technical/trade schools most often have strategic plans, albeit of varying quality and depth. Public sector organizations may or may not have a strategic plan based on their level of origin.

THE GOVERNMENT RESULTS PERFORMANCE ACT OF 1993

The Government Results Performance Act of 1993 (GRPA) directed all federal Departments and Agencies to have functional strategic plans; including Goals, Objectives, Evaluation Plans; descriptions of their strategic environment; and a planning scope of five years with a requirement to update and revise the strategic plan every three years. The GRPA forced many federal government elements to envelop strategic planning into their routine business practices. Where would you guess the GRPA 1993 directed such strategic plans to be submitted—you guessed it correctly, the Director of the Office of Management & Budget and the US Congress, the ultimate resource $$$ creators. This link between strategic plans and the resourcing/budget source is founded in solid principle.

As late as 1995, two years after the inception of GRPA 1993, the Department of Defense did not have one comprehensive Strategic Plan, rather a complex amalgam of strategic processes miserably *almost-linked* with titles such as; Defense Planning Guidance; Joint Strategic Capabilities Plan (JSCP); Contingency Planning Guidance (CPG); Joint Strategic Planning System (JSPS); Joint Strategy Review Process (JSR); National Military Strategy Document; Chairman's Program Assessment (CPA); Unified Command Plan (UCP);

Joint Requirements Oversight Council (JROC); Chairman's Program Recommendation (CPR). These products, councils and assessments were all part of just one federal Department, the Department of Defense's strategic *effort*.

THE QUALITY OF STRATEGIC PLANS VARIES GREATLY

Separate governmental entities at the state level may have a strategic plan, although continuity of strategic direction from department-to-department where such plans do exist is episodic. Likewise, the quality and scope of state-level governmental strategic plans is hit-or-miss at best.

My experience includes a rather diverse review of state-level governmental strategic plans from numerous states. Rather than identify specific States and Departments I will offer generic comparisons only. I am not attempting to kick sand in any one's face, rather to provide a feel for the varying scope of Strategic Plans I have reviewed. One large state-level Department with over 9,000 employees has a one page Strategic Plan merely outlining their Vision, Mission, Values and basic Goals. Another state-level department in another State had a strategic plan of three pages, one page of which was the Departmental Director's letter of distribution and yet another State-level department has a rather comprehensive 12 page strategic plan. The length of the strategic plan is not at issue here, however it does correlate to depth and quality much of the time. My point is this gamut runs from very poor to excellent strategic plans, with little common thread.

In my research I failed to find one State that has fair-to-good strategic plans throughout all departments, or has linked such fragmentary plans with common strategic guidance. In all my research I only found one state-level department that had metrics associated with every strategic Objective, a review cycle, published updates and automated metrics exported to every employee. That particular agency had also competed in the Malcolm Baldridge Quality Award competition in their state and earned the Malcolm Baldridge *Quality Leadership Award of Excellence* defeating large Universities, Fortune 500 manufacturers and healthcare conglomerates. Clearly much more can be done to improve the usefulness and value of Strategic Plans in state government.

THE MOST COMMON REASONS STRATEGIC PLANS FAIL

Many organizations that invested the efforts to craft a Strategic Plan, simply have abandoned their plans and they became bad memories of leadership and staff time wasted.

In my experience, **the single largest reason Strategic Plans fail within an organization has to be obsolescence**. And to be clear here, actually most often the organization has failed their Strategic Plan, not vice a versa. Simply, the organization failed to revise and update the Strategic Plan they so painstakingly crafted. The organization's strategic environment had changed, in some cases rather dramatically, yet little or no effort was made to *maintain* the Strategic Plan.

In organizations where a modest effort was made to keep the Strategic Plan current, reflective of a dynamic strategic environment and the Strategic Plan still failed the strategic desires, the most common root-cause can be attributed to **a lack of linkage to the organization's budgetary process**. Simply, targeted strategic Objectives were not resourced at a level, which allowed for or created their success.

The tertiary reason for strategic plans failing, or being ignored or abandoned in organizations, is the lack of an **effective measuring system** to gage strategic plan progress. These absent metrics fail to engender senior-leader stewardship and management of the strategic direction.

Finally, the fourth most common reason I fou.. strategic planning fails as a process within organizations, **a poor linkage between major sub-elements of an organization**. This failure usually occurred in organizations segmented by geography or leader-centric division. A simple lacking of organizational continuity.

MOST COMMON REASONS FOR FAILURES IN STRATEGIC PLANNING

- Failing to revise and update the Strategic Plan as the strategic environment changes.
- Absence of a clear linkage to the organizational budgetary or resource process.
- Absence of an understandable and meaningful measuring or metrics process associated with strategic Objectives.
- A lack of understanding how to link the strategic direction and guidance throughout a fragmentary organization, such as a vertical or horizontal organizational architecture.

WHO FAILED WHOM?

Let's clarify the vernacular, the relationships and failures so everyone understands. Technically speaking strategic plans rarely fail — usually the *organization fails* the Strategic Plan. As the gentleman, a few slips away from my boat in Ft. Lauderdale told me, we had both just endured 8 long days aboard our yachts during the 2004 Hurricane Frances, *"My unsinkable Boston Whaler dinghy was severely damaged and washed away by the torrents…and I believe it as my fault, I failed that great little boat."* He had regrettably tied his dinghy, on too short of painter, to a tree. Had the little boat been stored correctly ashore or given greater lead, she may have weathered the hurricane and survived intact. It was an unforgettable 8 days, yet I learned a valuable lesson from my dockside neighbor that treacherous day. *He* had failed that well designed, well built, ready-for-action vessel — the small boat had not failed him.

Other common reasons I find for organizations failing in strategic planning are not as great in number but remain a common theme among clients.

USING THE WRONG FACILITATOR

Hiring a facilitator not specifically trained or experienced in strategic planning or using an internal facilitator. Strategic planning requires a particular sequence of development. Key links have to be built, by the strategic planning group, which then create foundations for follow-on elements. The facilitator must understand how the products of the prioritized SWOT analysis generate the 'where we are now' location for movement towards the Vision, the ultimate 'where we want to be' location. Strategies must be customized for specific strategic Objectives, so when accomplished collectively meet the entirety of the strategic Goal, leaving nothing amiss. Metrics must be both understandable and meaningful to all readers, not just to experts within the organization and they should create a basis for decision-making by senior leaders. The facilitator must understand, the criticality for developing organizational Values lies within the *observable demonstrated behaviors* people can associate with those Values.

Almost all organizations have staffers with some experience or training in group facilitation. A common pitfall is using this internal asset just because they are available, known to the strategic planning team and naturally, less costly. This is a near-sighted shortcut. For numerous reasons, this perceived bargain rarely bears fruit. Internal facilitators often don't have the objectivity to work closely with senior leaders, especially during embarrassing revelations. Many have little experience in *coaching up* where senior leaders require coaching and guiding — with respect, courtesy and the delicate balance of respecting the CEO's authority. Additionally, few are trained in both facilitation and strategic planning. The right external facilitator can provide both of these experiential elements, in addition to providing real world experience from other organizations. I know some readers will assume my findings reflect my own facilitation and consulting perspective, a sour-grapes kind of shot at those organizations trying to proctor their own process. I am only relaying to my clients and readers what I have observed — some of these same organizations contact me after attempting their own facilitation — by then all of the senior leaders are frustrated. Restoration efforts with these groups can be ugly. Everyone wants results and senior leaders are exhausted with previous efforts. Believe me, hire a professional with the right credentials and enjoy the strategic planning process.

THE LACK OF A FACILITATOR

Of course many failures can be attributed to instances where no facilitator was hired. In these cases, one of the senior leaders adopts the responsibility for organizing the strategic planning efforts and immediately flies the strategic planning effort into the ground — in just three short meetings! It would be humorous if so much wasn't at stake.

TAKING THE SHORTCUT

I have observed several organizations fail with strategic planning because the strategic planning team decided to adopt a 'shortcut methodology' for development. Often in such cases, one of the senior leaders decides to omit or combine a few steps based on their previous strategic planning experience, often in the interest of saving time. Ouch! This is almost always disastrous and usually due to a lack of understanding how each Step of the strategic planning process is linked to other Steps. Great intentions although, well you know about the "road to hell is paved with good intentions." The strategic planning development Steps I have outlined in this text have proven themselves — IF there was a better way, I'd be using it.

INATTENTION OR THE LACK OF STRATEGIC FOCUS

Operational taskings are always tugging at the heels of senior (strategic) leaders. In a similar way, so are middle managers, usually with operational challenges in hand. Senior leaders, unlike middle managers of the operational realm, must spend the majority of their organizational time in the strategic realm. This is difficult to do and often requires formal strategic coaching to become effective. Strategic leaders have almost always *paid their organizational dues* to achieve their position in the organization. There is a natural gravitational-pull on people to gravitate to their comfort zones. Failing to maintain their attentions in the strategic realm, many senior leaders spend much of their daily routine *back* in the operational realm. This lack of strategic focus results in the comforts of, 'perfecting yesterday' and failing to identify opportunities to *progress* the organization. Simply, senior leaders fall back to their comfort zones of acting as operational leaders, thereby leaving 'no one at the controls' of the organization's *strategic* helm. This same failing can be observed in peewee soccer teams as everyone chases the ball, creating bumblebee groupings.

ORGANIZATIONAL SUB-ELEMENT FRAGMENTATION

Of the four primary reasons for strategic planning failing in organizations, as outlined previously in this chapter, the first three are quite self explanatory. The fourth reason requires some clarification;

> *"A lack of understanding how to link the strategic direction and guidance throughout a fragmentary organization, either vertical or horizontal."*

Here is an example that illustrates the proper method for connecting the *strategic direction* of a fragmentary (in this case, horizontal) organization, in this example the Nation's Army National Guard's many elements. While each Army National Guard organization belongs to their respective State's Governor, these same organizations are also an integral part of the total US Army. To properly align a horizontal organization (having more than one central leader), sharing the greater organization's **Vision** is the correct way to link together the fragmentary units (in this example, States). In many organizations, the Values are also common for all elements.

Where an organization is of vertical design (one central leader) it is possible to encompass all subordinate elements under a single holistic Strategic Plan. For example, if the Army National Guard were all organized under just one leader (i.e., the Chief, Joint National Guard Bureau) we might expect such vertical alignment under one comprehensive unified Strategic Plan, as in one large pyramid. However, because the National Guard is a horizontal organization, actually more a 'stretched-horizontal' organization, (having multiple central leaders, i.e., state Governors), the

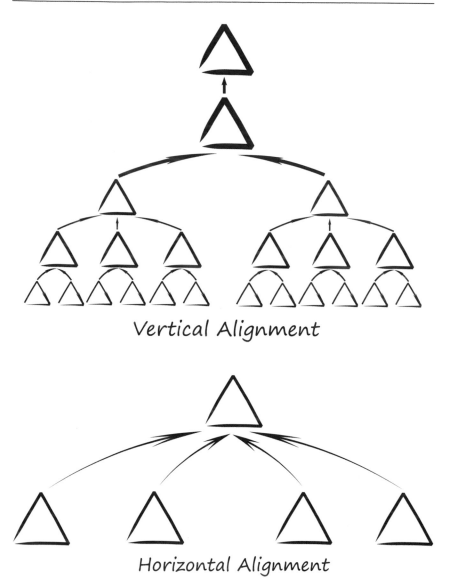

Vertical Alignment

Horizontal Alignment

proper methodology for creating organizational alignment is to share a common **Vision**. Not necessarily a Vision that is identical in wording, rather a common **Vision** regarding *content and sentiment*. **Vision** is the correct linking-process for aligning elements of horizontal or stretched-horizontal organizations. In this way subordinate elements can create

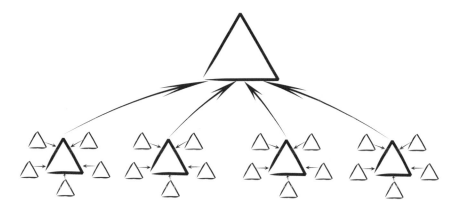

Stretched Horizontal Alignment

their own customized strategic plans, thus achieving organizational *alignment* while still recognizing multiple leadership, geographic, cultural and resource influences.

The US Army goes one step further to ensure all three US Army components (active US Army, Army National Guard and the US Army Reserve) are adequately linked with the US Army by sharing common Values. Imagine linking and creating strategic direction for an organization with almost a million members?

Vertical organizations that are fragmented by geography have the same potential for failing to maintain a unified strategic direction as horizontal organizations.

Strategic directional continuity is fragile and therefore requires deliberate efforts to establish, reinforce and sustain by strategic leaders. Frequent senior leader visitation, visual aids like posters and other graphic reminders and face-to-face town hall discussions are great investments in preserving this directional continuity, a key ingredient of organizational success.

REMINDERS—IN A NUTSHELL

The 11 Steps outlined in this text require your strategic planning team to complete these 17 actions to develop a Strategic Plan.

1. Conduct an **Environmental Scan,** develop staff estimates of impacts on the organization.

2. Hire an **external facilitator** trained in strategic planning.

3. Craft the organization's **Vision, Mission, and Values.** This is a huge process—but critical foundation elements.

4. Conduct a **SWOT Analysis.** Lengthy discussion with cross-functional impacts considered for every element.

5. *Prioritize* **the SWOT** elements based upon each element's impact on your mission and organization — a relative ranking, what's significant, what isn't.

6. **Write Alternative Future statements** defining what will probably happen to your organization— based on what you know and projections.

7. **Develop bridge-statements** (gap analysis), things that you believe absolutely MUST happen to 'take your organization from where they are—to where it needs to go.'

8. **Affinity Exercise.** Re-group your bridge-statements, think themes. These group themes, after grouping and re-stating become the strategic Goals.

9. For each Goal, **list the 'critical imperatives'** that absolutely must be accomplished in order to accomplish the overall Goal—restated these will become strategic Objectives. See #10.

10. **Re-write these 'critical imperatives' using the SMART criteria.** These become the subordinate Strategic Objectives.

11. **Develop strategies for each Strategic Objective.** Ideally 1 or 2 , no more than 3. Strategies specify 'how' to pursue Objectives.

12. **Develop the metrics** (identify elements of measure) for the Strategic Objectives. Should include a time element + 2 or more other measures.

13. **Develop the Target or Success Matrix** by creating a simple matrix portraying all strategic Objectives and their respective completion dates. Then identify by Year-columns which Objectives are targeted for each year.

14. Develop a cyclic Strategic Plan *review process*— should be cyclic, strategic plans are dynamic, not static—strategic environments change.

15. Develop guidance to subordinate small team's for **Action Plans.** Specify responsibility, milestones, what success looks like. Employ *tracking*.

16. **Deployment** *process* **to all stakeholders,** not just an event. CEO lead, delivered and marketed.

17. Procedurally and systemically **link your Strategic Plan to the organizational budgetary process.** Budget/resourcing process must reflect the priorities for strategic Objectives, ensure critical steps are well resourced.

EPILOGUE

The strategic planner must understand how the various and numerous building blocks support a dynamic Strategic Plan. While my text focuses on the actual development of a strategic plan, more a process-centric tutorial, it is not enough to leave the reader's understanding of how the building blocks complement one another to chance. I purposely chose not to attempt to explain and clarify why many organizations do not have viable strategic plans. I also elected not to market or over-sell the Malcolm Baldrige quality initiatives because they speak for themselves. It is widely known by business gurus, organizations using Malcolm Baldrige quality practices outperform their counterparts by a vast margin.

I do want readers to fully comprehend how the various elements and numerous relationships involved in strategic planning link together. Vision, Mission and Values provide a necessary foundation for creating a base from which to launch organizational direction. In a rudimentary way this triad presents the Why (Vision), the What (Mission) and the How (Values). We develop these early in the strategic planning process precisely because of their foundational purpose.

115

Strategic direction remains that conceptual azimuth an organization proceeds along, whether accurate and correct for it or not. This directional tangent is modified repeatedly by Goals and actual performance, by leveraging a workforce collectively, not individually and through fueling the workforce's synergy to accomplish the correct Objectives using the most effective Strategies. Only time, history and thorough analysis can validate the organizational trajectory as the ideal one. It is important to understand a correct and proper strategic direction can provide the nucleus for organizational alignment. Myriad authors and critics claim organizational alignment as the utopian panacea for organizational excellence. Only organizations can determine this for themselves.

I profess, we as senior leaders should always generate synergy in a disjointed way. Motivating juniors at every opportunity remains a charter responsibility of every leader. Mentoring less experienced team members is always and should always be a primacy role for leaders. Setting a correct example by demonstrating role-model behaviors creates more attention and says more to associates than all the newsletters, speeches and reminders any of us can provide. Team synergy will always be generated and sustained in the same way as the confluence of great rivers.

Organizational alignment will be achieved only when several key elements settle into a working relationship which can flex and bind organizations together in a growing way. Organizational behavior, leader's behavior, and associates' behaviors must complement and demonstrate the organizational Values. Actual performance must contain self-improvement methodologies, self-directed initiatives and be accomplished by team members fully empowered to achieve their greatest potential—because of or in spite of the organization. The organizational Vision must be seen and understood by all contributors to that accomplishment, both inside and outside the organization, by feeling ownership and pride during the journey.

I have assembled this collection of best-practices from my experience with successful clients, achieving those things codified in their strategic plans, developed using my techniques and processes. The weak links in all organizations lie in their discipline and dedication to these practices and processes. The ever changing, ever evolving strategic environment demands strategic planning based on constant revisions and updating. Only a flexible process, executed in a disciplined and vigilant way will keep the strategic direction properly aimed on the moving target — the Vision. Organizational alignment will describe the path to achievement and be the hallmark of weaving together these diverse actions and concepts.

REFERENCES & RESOURCES

Armstrong, Frank A., *Memos To Management*, New York, NY, Stein and Day, 1974

Army Directorate, National Guard Bureau, *Our Future Is Here Long Range Plan 1993-2012*, Washington D.C., National Guard Bureau, 1993

Babich, Pete, *Hoshin Handbook, Focus and Link Activities Throughout the Organization*, Poway, CA, Total Quality Engineering, Inc., 1996

Behn, Robert, D., *The Psychological Barriers To Performance Management: Or Why Isn't Everyone Jumping On the Performance-Management Bandwagon?*, Cambridge, MA, 2002

Behn, Robert, D., *Why Measure Performance? Different Purposes Require Different Measures*, Cambridge, MA, Harvard University John F. Kennedy School of Government, 2002

Belasco, James A., Stead, Jerre, *Soaring With The Phoenix*, New York, NY, Warner Books Inc., 1999

BG Denson, Kerry G., *Wisconsin Army National Guard Strategic Plan*, Madison, WI, Department of Military Affairs, Wisconsin, 2003

BG McDaniel, Michael C., *Securing Michigan 2010*, Lansing, MI, Department of Military & Veterans Affairs, State of Michigan, 2006

BG Seely, Ronald Y., *Michigan Air National Guard Strategic Plan 2002-2006*, Lansing, MI, Joint Force HQs Michigan, US Air Force, 2002

BG Taylor, Robert V., *Michigan Vision 2005: The Strategic Plan for the Michigan Army National Guard Compendium 2004*, Lansing, MI, Department of Military & Veterans Affairs, State of Michigan, 2004

BG Taylor, Robert V., *Michigan Vision 2005: The Strategic Plan for the Michigan Army National Guard Compendium 2003*, Lansing, MI, Department of Military & Veterans Affairs, State of Michigan, 2003

BG Taylor, Robert V., *Michigan Vision 2005: The Strategic Plan for the Michigan Army National Guard Compendium 2002*, Lansing, MI, Department of Military & Veterans Affairs, State of Michigan, 2002

BG Taylor, Robert V., *Michigan Vision 2005: The Strategic Plan for the Michigan Army National Guard*, Lansing, MI, Department of Military & Veterans Affairs, State of Michigan, 2001

BG Taylor, Robert V., *Michigan Vision 2010: The Strategic Plan for the Michigan Army National Guard*, Lansing, MI, Department of Military & Veterans Affairs, State of Michigan, 2005

Brandt, Steven C., *Strategic Planning In Emerging Companies*, Reading, MA, Addison-Wesley, 1987

BrigGen Cutler, Thomas, *127th Fighter Wing Year 2000 Strategic Plan*, Mt Clemens, MI, Department of Military & Veterans Affairs, State of Michigan, 2000

Center for Army Lessons Learned, *Newsletter No. 95-12, Military Decision Making: Abbreviated Planning*, Ft Leavenworth, KS, U.S. Army Training and Doctrine Command, 1997

City of Waterloo, *Strategic Plan 1999-2000*, Waterloo, Ontario, Canada, City of Waterloo, 1999

COL Giddis, Joseph A., *NGPEC Strategic Plan 2000*, North Little Rock, AR, National Guard Bureau, Washington D.C., 2000

Col Heaton, Kencil J., *110th Fighter Wing Strategic Plan 2000-2004*, Battle Creek, MI, Department of Military & Veterans Affairs, State of Michigan, 2000

Col Heaton, Kencil J., *110th Fighter Wing Strategic Plan 2001-2005*, Battle Creek, MI, Department of Military & Veterans Affairs, State of Michigan, 2001

Col Heaton, Kencil J., *Michigan Air National Guard Strategic Plan 2005-2009*, Lansing, MI, Joint Force HQs Michigan, US Air Force, 2005

Command Group, *Strategic Business Plan, Ft. McCoy, WI*, Ft. McCoy, WI, HQs US Army FORSCOM, 2001

Cottrell, David. *Listen Up Leader!*, Dallas, TX, CornerStone Leadership Institute, 200

Covey, Steven R. PhD, *Unleashing Human Potential*, Franklin Covey Co., 2001

Department of Command, Leadership and Management, *Strategic Leadership Primer*, Carlisle, PA, U.S. Army War College, 1998

Department of Management and Budget, *Strategic Plan 2000*, Lansing, MI, State of Michigan, 2000

Field Manual 22-100, *Army Leadership, Be, Know, Do*, Washington D.C., HQs US Army, 1999

Field Manual 22-101, *Leadership Counseling*, Washington D.C., HQs US Army, 1985

Field Manual, 100-14, *Risk Management*, Washington, D.C., HQs US Army, 1998

Finzel, Hans, *The Top Ten Mistakes Leaders Make*, Colorado Springs, CO, Cook Communications Ministries, 2000

Fogg, C. Davis, *Team-Based Strategic Planning: A Complete Guide to Structuring, Facilitating and Implementing the Process*, New York, NY, AMACOM American Management Association, 1994

Gitlow, Howard, Gitlow, Shelly, Oppenheim, Alan, Oppenheim, Rosa, *Tools and Methods for the Improvement of Quality*, Homewood, IL, Richard Irwin, INC., 1989

Gross, T. Scott, *Leading Your Positively Outrageous Service Team*, New York, NY, Mastermedia Limited, 1994

Haimann, Theo., Hilgert, Raymond L., *Supervision: Concepts and Practices of Management*, Cincinnati, OH, South-Western, 1972

Harvey, Eric L., Lucia, Alexander D., *144 Ways To Walk the Talk*, Dallas, TX, Performance Publishing Co., undated

Hersey, Paul, Blanchard, Ken, *Management of Organizational Behavior Utilizing Human Resources*, Englewood Cliffs, NJ, 1982

Kaplan, Robert S., Norton, David P., *The Balanced Scorecard*, Boston, MA, Harvard Business School Press, 1996

King, John H. Jr., *HDS Services 2004-2007 Strategic Business Plan*, Farmington Hills, MI, HDS Services, 2004

Kouzes, James M., Posner, Barry Z., *Leadership Practices Inventory*, San Francisco, CA, Pfeiffer, 2003

Kouzes, James M., Posner, Barry Z., *The Leadership Challenge*, San Francisco, CA, Jossey-Bass, 2002

Langley, Gerald J., Nolan, Kevin M., Nolan, Thomas W., Norman, Clifford L., Provost, Lloyd P., *The Improvement Guide A Practical Approach to Enhancing Organizational Performance*, San Francisco, CA, Jossey-Bass, 1996

Lee, Sang, Shim, Jung, *Micro Management Science*, Dubuque, IA, Wm. C. Brown, 1986

Lovelace, Douglas C., Jr., Young, Thomas-Durell, *U.S. Department of Defense Strategic Planning: The Missing Nexus*, Carlisle, PA, The Strategic Studies Institute, U.S. Army War College, 1995

LTG Blum, H Steven, *National Guard Bureau Strategic Plan (DRAFT)*, Washington D.C., National Guard Bureau, 2006

MG Denson, Kerry G., *Future Plan 2000-2005*, Madison, WI, Wisconsin Department of Military Affairs, 1999

MG Ingram, William E., *North Carolina National Guard Strategic Plan*, Raleigh, NC, The Adjutant General's Office, 2004

MG Ivany, Robert R., *United States Army War College 2010 Strategic Plan*, Carlisle, PA, US Army War College, undated

MG Umbarger, R. Martin, *Indiana National Guard 5 Year Strategic Plan*, Indianapolis, IN, Joint Force HQs Indiana, US Army/US Air Force, 2005

Michigan Department of Agriculture, *Strategic Plan 1999*, Lansing, MI, State of Michigan, 1999

Michigan Department of Civil Service, *Strategic Plan 2003-2005*, Lansing, MI, State of Michigan, 2003

Michigan Department of Transportation, *2006 Strategic Plan*, Lansing, MI, State of Michigan, 2006

Murphy, Robert M., PhD, *Managing Strategic Change: An Executive Overview of Management*, Carlisle Barracks, PA, U.S. Army War College, undated

National Guard Professional Education Center, *Performance Measurement and Practical Applications*, Little Rock, AR, National Guard Bureau, 1999

Northeast Counterdrug Training Center, *Northeast Counterdrug Training Center Strategic Plan*, Pennsylvania National Guard, Philadelphia, PA, 2000

Office of Performance Excellence, *Strategic Plan FY 1999-2000*, Lansing, MI, State of Michigan, 1999

Patton, Bobby R., Giffin, Kim, *Decision-Making Group Interaction*, New York, NY, Harper & Row, 1978

Peters, Tom, *The Circle of Innovation*, 1999

Scherkenback, William W., *Deming's Road to Continual Improvement*, Knoxville, TN, SPC Press, 1991

Scherkenback, William W., *The Deming Route to Quality and Productivity Roadmaps and Roadblocks*, Rockville, MD, Mercury Publishing Services, 1994

Shafe, Jim, *How To Develop an Attitude for Success*, Atlanta, GA, Career Training Concepts, 1988

Sholtes, Peter R., *The Leader's Handbook A Guide To Inspiring Your People and Managing the Daily Workflow*, New York, NY, McGraw-Hill, 1998

Sholtes, Peter R., *The Team Handbook*, Madison, WI, Joiner Associates Inc., 1988

Strickland, A.G., *How To Get Action*, West Nyack, NY, Parker Publishing Company, Inc., 1975

Sullivan, Gordon R., Harper, Michael V., *Hope Is Not A Method*, New York, NY, Broadway Books, 1996

The Adjutant General of California, *Vision 2020*, Sacramento, CA, California National Guard, 1989

The Adjutant General, *Georgia Department of Defense Strategic Plan 2004-2009*, Atlanta, GA, Georgia Dept of Defense Office of the Adjutant General, 2003

The Adjutant General, *Puerto Rico National Guard Strategic Plan 2002*, Puerto Rico, 2002

Tichy, Noel M., Devanna, Mary Anne, *The Transformational Leader*, New York, NY, John Wiley & Sons, 1986

Walton, Mary, *Deming Management At Work*, New York, NY, Putnam Publishing Group, 1991

Wells, Denise, Doherty, Linda M. PhD, *A Handbook for Strategic Planning*, undated

Wyoming Military Department, *Strategic Plan*, Cheyenne, WY, Wyoming Military Department, 2000

Young, Ronald G., *Strategic Plan 2001 The Ohio Army National Guard*, State of Ohio, 2001

CROCK-POT BRUNSWICK STEW

1 can (14.5oz) diced tomatoes

1 can (6oz) tomato paste

3 cups chicken or squirrel, cooked and cubed

1 ½ cups frozen, sliced okra (thawed)

1 cup corn kernels, frozen (thawed) or fresh

1 cup chopped onion

1 bay leaf

1 teaspoon salt

¼ teaspoon dried rosemary, crushed

¼ teaspoon dried oregano, crushed

1 teaspoon pepper

1 dash ground cloves

2 ½ cups chicken stock

In a slow cooker, combine tomatoes and tomato paste; stir to blend. Add chicken or squirrel, sliced okra, corn, onion, bay leaf, salt, rosemary, oregano, pepper and cloves. Stir in chicken stock. Cover and cook on 'low' setting for 5-6 hours.

PAGE 36 REFERENCE TO A STRATEGIC PLANNING SESSION:

I define a productive strategic planning session as a six hour period, dedicated to only strategic planning, isolated from all other distractions, working group discussion. This would be facilitated by an external facilitator with the full attention of the working group members. Periodic breaks of 10 minutes per hour allow sufficient time to place telephone calls, refill beverages, etc. All electronic devices i.e., computers, PDAs, cellular telephones, beepers, etc., would remain outside the actual meeting room.

SUCCESS MATRIX EXAMPLE FROM PAGE 58

#	Objective	FY10	FY11	FY12	FY13
1.1	Sdfethrhut dfertij ase wr mkuiyt ger by April 15, 2010	X			
1.2	Olpiuhn fregrtru xsaxz cd-fert not later than October 15, 2009	X			
1.3	bmngjyi ngjthup, mfips efui nks by February 1, 2011		X		
1.4	Annually ase wr mkuiyt ger-fvb et, uionelpiuhn fregrtru xsaxz by July 30th.	X	X	X	X

Subject Index

About the Author

Colonel (ret) Berri K. Meyers B.A., M.S.S., is President of b.k. meyers & associates, LLC, a Michigan-based consulting firm. He is a progressive executive coach, advisor, author and speaker. Berri's objective assessments have guided myriad public and private-sector leaders through the challenges of building and maintaining strategic direction. Berri has facilitated the development of countless Strategic Plans for military, business and government clients.

Berri has made over 150 presentations on strategic planning, quality initiatives and customer service. He

has written numerous articles, appeared on radio talk shows and is a frequent keynote speaker. His passion for excellence generates excitement and team direction for moving organizations forward. Berri has lead organizations through numerous Malcolm Baldrige Quality competitions, achieving unprecedented awards.

Berri completed his graduate studies at the prestigious US Army War College and has transitioned from 36 years of military service. He delivers a straightforward approach for weaving the proven planning processes he developed with the realities of labor relations, employee morale and real organizational growth.

Berri can re-energize and coach the strategic direction for your organization. Working with your senior leaders he can assist you in reaching your organizational Vision. To learn how b.k. meyers & associates can maximize your organizational alignment, visit bkmeyersandassociates.com

b.k. meyers & associates, LLC
517-322-0116
berrimeyers@comcast.net
www.bkmeyersandassociates.com

NOTES

NOTES

23.95
3
71.85
.06
421.10

Four ways to order:

Strategic Planning: Clean Up In Aisle 4!

Phone
Please provide a shipping address, quantity, Credit Card # & Exp date, contact tel #
Call 1.517.322.0116 EST

Website
Visit us online 24/7
www.bkmeyersandassociates.com

Mail
Use order form below
b.k. meyers & associates, LLC
4734 Thornapple Lane
Lansing, Michigan 48917-4433

FAX
Use order form below
517.322.0116

Discounts available for orders of 25 books or more!

Call us today! 1.517.322.0116

Name: DAVE WENGLEROWSKI C/O STANTON & ASSOC., INC.

Address: 714 W. MICHIGAN AVE.

City: JACKSON **State:** MI **Zip:** 49201

Phone: (517) 784-4094 (Ext.112) **Fax:** (517) 784-6344

E-mail: Dave.W@stantonnet.com

Credit Card #: _____ **Exp. Date:** _____

U.S. Funds only   Book Price: $23.95   Plus MI Tax: 6%

Shipping and Handling:

U.S.: $4.00 for first book and $1.00 for each additional book.

International: $9.00 for first book and $5.00 for each additional book.

	Quantity	Cost/Book	Total
Strategic Planning: Clean Up in Aisle 4!	3	$23.95	$71.85
Shipping			6.00
6% MI Tax			$4.21
Total			$82.06

FOUR WAYS TO ORDER:

STRATEGIC PLANNING: CLEAN UP IN AISLE 4!

Phone Please provide a shipping address, quantity, Credit Card # & Exp date, contact tel # Call 1.517.322.0116 EST

Website Visit us online 24/7 www.bkmeyersandassociates.com

Mail Use order form below
b.k. meyers & associates, LLC
4734 Thornapple Lane
Lansing, Michigan 48917-4433

FAX Use order form below
517.322.0116

Discounts available for orders of 25 books or more!

Call us today! 1.517.322.0116

Name:_____

Address:_____

City: _____ **State:**_____ **Zip:**_____

Phone: _____ **Fax:** _____

E-mail:_____

Credit Card #:_____ **Exp. Date:** _____

U.S. Funds only   Book Price: $23.95   Plus MI Tax: 6%

Shipping and Handling:

U.S.: $4.00 for first book and $1.00 for each additional book.

International: $9.00 for first book and $5.00 for each additional book.

	Quantity	Cost/Book	Total
STRATEGIC PLANNING: CLEAN UP IN AISLE 4!		$23.95	
Shipping			
6% MI Tax			
Total			